702

DATE DUE

Sept.27/93		

GAYLORD   PRINTED IN U.S.A

THE
Poor Man's Prayer

THE POOR MAN'S PRAYER

The Story of
Credit Union Beginnings

By George Boyle

PALM PUBLISHERS · MONTREAL
HELICON PRESS · BALTIMORE, MARYLAND

To
EDMUND A. BRASSET, M.D.

Preface

Once I had heard the stories and legends surrounding the name of Alphonse Desjardins in the province of Quebec, Canada, this book had to be written. The thought of this man haunted me; in his simplicity, in his awakened social conscience fifty years ago, in his faith, fearlessness and selfless dedication, he was an interesting human character in his own right.

When added to that was the tremendous aftermath of his life work and teaching, the spread of the credit union idea to nearly all parts of the world, I felt sure that here was one worthy to live on in the hearts of men.

His adventure was in the field of spiritual values and ideas. His master theme was that all men have a social duty. He called it an everlasting duty. The span of thirty years since his death only serves to light up the truth of his words.

The purpose of this book, then, is that the courageous and achieving dead may live again to cheer on the living.

G. B.

Foreword

BY

THOMAS W. DOIG

*Managing Director, Credit Union
National Association, Inc.*

HERE is an absorbing, warm-with-life story, told with dramatic and narrative skill.

It is heartening to know that this is a true story, told by a conscientious scholar. Surely all people concerned with human progress will find encouragement and inspiration from the life here revealed to us as so human and yet so saintly.

Naturally, credit union people who honor Desjardins as the founder of the credit union movement on the North American continent are particularly moved by this story. It is good for us to be reminded, by the example of Desjardins himself, that credit unions are organizations of people to obtain democratic answers to their own grave economic problems. As our credit unions grow in size and numbers they increasingly need such examples if they are not to lose the spirit which motivated their founders, and which is their reason for being. The human factor, so well expressed in these pages, is the all-important factor.

I am happy to know that this credit union book comes to the reader from the same distinguished publishing company, at about the same time, as *Credit for the Millions, the Story of Credit Unions*, by Richard Y. Giles. These two books rightly go together. Each will increase the reader's satisfaction in the other. I commend them both to all who are searching for ways people can better unite to further their own well-being.

THE
Poor Man's Prayer

Chapter 1

KNOCK, knock, knock!

The visitor was standing outside the house of Alphonse Desjardins in Lévis, P.Q.

Mon dieu! Someone was at the door again.

Dorimène, before she had backed away from the oven on the big stove in her kitchen and closed its door upon the family roast, felt that she knew what the rapping was about. She wiped her hands and smoothed her apron.

"Adrienne," she called to her daughter, who had just the moment before come in from school and was sidling up to the warmth of the kitchen stove. "Keep an eye on that roast, dear."

As Dorimène walked through the house to answer the door on this afternoon in midwinter, there was brooding in her downcast eyes.

A savings and loan bank for the neighbors! A little society. All very fine—but what a bother! There was no end to it.

A *caisse populaire*, her husband called it. Indeed, but who counted her anxious moments? And they had already endured so much together in this house.

The memory of it swept over her: the building of the house, first of all—when the contractor had let them down, and they had no suitable place in which to live; then the long illness that had come upon him, making him look like a walking skeleton; losing his job at last and their struggle to support the growing family; and worst of all, his high notion of starting the *caisse populaire* as a means to teach the people thrift. Their other troubles had ended; of this there was no end. . . .

At the door, stood a little boy of the neighborhood of Lévis, Emile Poulin.

He was holding something tightly clenched in a dirty fist.

"I have come with ten cents," he said.

"Well, now, Emile!" Dorimène showed him in to the small room which Alphonse Desjardins had had set aside for the affairs of the *caisse populaire* that he had started. There was a table, a desk, a few chairs, and a cabinet.

"It is for the *caisse*," he continued.

"That is very smart of you, Emile."

He shifted his feet; his eyes glowed with the thought of making a clean breast of all his virtues:

"I have given up candy," he said as if he didn't quite believe it himself.

At that she patted his tousled head. "Such a good boy! Now, aren't you!"

"For Lent," Emile amended, already a little aghast at the recklessness of his conversion.

She took the coin and made an entry in the book.

"Papa tells me if I save now there will be more money for later on," Emile said.

"Yes, of course, and you're a smart boy to do it."

She gave him a parting pat and he was gone.

Emile had given up candy for Lent, and was saving ten cents quite often. And it was all because of the *caisse populaire*. Well, the little bank had already brought together in goodly amount the savings of some of the people of the neighborhood, though not five years had passed since it started.

But it was not for her, this handling of other people's money and keeping accounts. When Alphonse was home he did all that.

When she came back to the kitchen it pleased her to get the good smell of cooking food. Ah, that was real and satisfying and something that didn't take any book entries.

Adrienne was bent over holding open the oven door. "I think it is done, Mama," she said.

"Good, Adrienne; let me see now."

"Was it someone again about the *caisse*?"

"Yes, little Emile."

"Humph?" said Adrienne in a tone of interrogation. And then:

"Mama, what is a *caisse populaire*?"

"Don't you know?"

"In a way, but——"

"It is something that your papa thought of to help the poor."

"Like when the little Vernier baby had the measles and they needed a stove to warm the room?"

"Yes, Papa Vernier had been putting little savings in the *caisse*. So he could borrow and buy the stove to keep baby warm."

"Mama, how did our papa think of that?"

Dorimène took out the roast and put it on the kitchen table. Adrienne followed her. She was a bright-faced girl with eager eyes and wore a long black dress and laced shoes. She stood at the end of the table waiting for her mother to answer.

Dorimène cut a small slice of the succulent pork and handed it to her daughter.

"Mm, that tastes good, Mama."

"Well, your papa saw how the poor suffer. And he thought and thought about it a long time. Then he read books about how people could save and put it all together and when someone needed it bad, loan it to him. They would have control of their savings themselves. Then he prayed——"

"He prayed?"

"Yes, he even made a prayer and wrote it down."

"Our papa made a prayer and wrote it down!" Adrienne's eyes stuck out with awe. She was silent for a moment before she said:

"Poor Papa, he must have wished so hard to do this when he wrote a prayer for it."

Dorimène turned her face away. She did not want Adrienne to see her own misgivings, her anxiety about the increasing work that the *caisse* was bringing to her.

That there was a prayer she knew. Alphonse had written it and put it away. And no one saw it.

"If he were only here to look after the *caisse!*" sighed Dorimène. "Every day they come——"

"And it makes you so busy, Mama!"

"All the money has to be kept—and put in a regular bank for safekeeping. Then there are the accounts to be kept straight. Everyone's deposits. There are loans, and then payments on loans. A whole batch of records to keep . . ."

"It is too much, Mama. With Papa away in Ottawa so long. But he will soon be home now and you can rest."

Dorimène looked indulgently at her daughter. She felt blessed in children.

But the thing that troubled her most she did not mention. The children must not know. There were persons around Lévis who were asking questions. Taking care of someone else's money was a responsibility, they said. It frightened her, this talk.

When Alphonse was home it was all right. He would take care of all this and there would be no question; it was because of his ideas and talking with his neighbors that they were bringing in their dimes and their dollars. Oh, if Alphonse were only home!

Knock, knock, knock!

Someone was at the door again.

Dorimène winced. Was no privacy left to them?

Her beauty now was not quite the same that used to bring Alphonse to Sorel to see and woo her more than twenty years previous. Then men would turn in her presence to look—as if they felt that hers was beauty to be acknowledged on the spot else the proper scale of values could not be maintained in the universe.

On this day in the house in Lévis, Dorimène was the mother of sons and daughters, the eldest of which were entering adulthood. The face was radiant above the full bosom; it was a face that knew anxiety, to be sure, but those anxieties were not the introverted notions of someone neurotic about neuroses. Dorimène's anxieties were exterior, as real and exterior as getting a pair of boots for her third youngest.

The thick auburn hair was graying at the temples, and her eyes, were eyes that have known the scald of tears, the stretching of a soul's faith and prayerful vigils. And there was an unconscious dignity suffusing the physical femininity.

What a succession of door-rapping there had been since *La Caisse Populaire de Lévis* was formed! She had had four years of it now. Some came regularly with their savings. Others didn't come at all. Others talked and sneered. More than once in the roundabout, telltale ways of gossip, she had heard the rumors:

"What a big idea it was that Alphonse Desjardins should take it into his head to start a bank in his own house! And himself away at Ottawa working as the *Hansard* reporter of the Commons half the time.

"He had an obsession, all right. He was a little mad. A fine thing, that! Something bad is sure to happen sooner or later. Just now you watch!"

At the very first she did not mind it so much. The little bank had had only twenty-six dollars at the beginning. But now, year by year, the sums were accumulating. In summer when Alphonse was home all the time, all was well.

He, the founder, knew all about it that was known; he kept the accounts; he could size up the loans and keep track of all the payments. It interested him and pleased him, that. He would always say: "Keep the money working." He would tend these accounts carefully like a gardener watching his plants and encouraging them to grow. To see the savings of the poor and the shiftless ones grow made him exult; it was a bank in their own hands.

Why had they always put the fruit of their thrift in someone else's hands? he would ask. Now the growing accounts were proof that what he had been preaching was right.

As the deposits grew, there was more to loan—on good character.

When he told her of certain shiftless ones who were saving regularly now, he could not control the excitement in his voice.

"Such men would never have saved in the ordinary bank," he said.

"It is something more than a matter of money, this, I tell you.

"This is, too, a power for the people that they have not been thinking about."

Living in harmony with every aspiration of her husband, she tried to feel his excitement at the prospect of the workers having a ready source of credit of their own. No need to tell her what one suffered when there was need in the family—a baby being born, or a grandmother to be laid away—happenings that one heard of every week in the neighborhood of this house in Lévis wherein Alphonse Desjardins had pondered, had planned and acted.

She had done everything possible to overcome her dislike of handling other people's money and keeping accounts, but without success. It was a burden, beyond doubt, and Alphonse was as anxious as she that some shift should be made to relieve her of it when he was away. With the small earnings so far, it was not possible to hire the services of anyone to take his place.

The society had been set up with a regular board of directors, a credit committee (to pass on loans), and a supervisory committee. While these members were sincere supporters of Alphonse's idea, they seldom had time to carry out extra functions, certainly not those of a competent treasurer. The actual keeping of the *caisse* had to be the appointed duty of someone who was always on the spot.

One idea had been that the bank would be open for deposits in the quarters of the Society of Artisans of Lévis on Monday, Wednesday and Saturday evenings. That took off some of the burden, but still it was found necessary to have it understood that deposits could be taken to the house of M. Desjardins during the day.

Then he thought of trying to get some man to take his place while he was away. It shouldn't be too hard, at first he had told her—not allowing that other persons did not have the same zeal he had for this work.

Together then they had looked at the list of the society's board of directors, canvassing each one in his mind for what part he might be able to play in the diverse and growing operations of the bank. But these good and helpful members, busy as they were with their everyday work of making a living, could not be counted upon for the type of service and experience that was required.

Always it had to be Dorimène—the good wife. She was the only stand-by. Always he had had to come back to her.

With an air of resignation that her household duties must wait, she pulled open the door to the one who had been knocking. There stood a man whom she recognized at once as one of the members of the *caisse*. He was clad in woodsman's boots and sheepskin coat. He was tanned, more with winter's wind than sun, and the deep breaths that came from his nostrils hung half frozen in the air and followed him through the doorway.

"*Bonjour*, Madame," he said. "I have come to make payment on my loan."

"Yes, M. Guillet, very well."

She ushered him into the room and turned up the account to Charles Guillet, Woodcutter.

Guillet's account was in good shape, she saw. Besides his share he had been making small deposits for some months. There had been regular payments upon his loan made the preceding fall in the amount of $200, purpose: to buy a team of horses with which he was hauling bobsled loads of firewood for the numerous wood-burning stoves used in the homes of Lévis. She often saw his team upon the streets. Yes, this was a good member, his loans paid regularly, unlike some that were slow in their repayments and caused uneasiness to her husband and herself as the volume of the banking operations expanded.

"Has it been a success, then, buying the new team?" she asked him, with the kindly but not intrusive interest that the Desjardins held toward the members of the *caisse*. He laid the bills upon the desk. She wrote his receipt and sat making the required entries.

"I am happy to say, Madame, it has been a good move from the start. When I think of what it was costing me when I borrowed money from a loan shark three years ago in order to buy my wood . . ." He made a bristling motion with his shoulders.

"How much did he charge you?"

She knew and liked this plain man. He was hard-working and rearing a young family. It gave her a warm inward glow to know that their *caisse* was helping him and his little ones, and that now the irritation and worry were forgotten.

"I did not try to figure it out myself," he said, "but I told one of my friends who is good at figures and he said that I had paid over sixty per cent. It was such that I could make no profit in my work. Now that one can have loans so cheap from the *caisse*, and dealing with one's own neighbors whom we know, it is more easy to be doing things."

"I am happy that you have been served," she said.

"I do not mind it that one has to borrow when a business has been set up just for that," he added.

"You are wise, M. Guillet. My husband has always said that there were some so foolishly proud that they would suffer in secret before they would borrow from ones they know. They'd sooner go to some stranger and be stuck."

"Or go to some banker, hat in hand and feeling like a sheep," said M. Guillet.

"Yes, and would you get it then? When they didn't know you?"

"It is not too soon that this *caisse* of M. Desjardins has been started," he said. "And I, for one, pay no attention to what some are saying . . ." his voice fell, as if apologetically.

"What is it that some are saying?" she asked, the blood in her cheeks.

"Oh, about the *caisse* failing. What if some of the borrowers did not pay their loans, and then the members might start taking out their shares and deposits? Even the money could be taken by someone in the *caisse*."

He stopped. Dorimène paled then suddenly and her hand trembled a little.

"Are these rumors believed by any number of the members, do you think?"

"It is hard to say." There was no assurance in his tone.

"Me—I always say when I am delivering wood at the houses and the question comes up, Will the *caisse* fail and our savings be lost? I say no. Have faith in M. Desjardins. He is a straight-thinking man, that one. There is too much gossip.

"One has said: 'Starting a bank—that is big business. That is for financiers. With much capital. Even sometimes they fail. It is not for an ordinary man to start a bank.'"

She felt her heart had missed a beat.

Was then, indeed, her husband an impractical dreamer entering into the complicated business of money, credit, and banking—a business that had always been the close patrimony of a select and almost anonymous few, working mysteriously behind gilded fronts in great stone buildings in the cities, assisted by trained clerks, and with nationwide and international connections? She sought to stifle the fear that troubled her.

"So that is what they are saying," she answered Guillet with but the slightest edge of defiance in her tones.

"You know, of course, that there are some who do not want to see such a bank succeed among our people," she told him.

He stared at her searchingly, for she had not succeeded completely in suppressing her agitation. He was torn between a sense of loyalty to the group that had helped him and doubts that had their origins in an age-old awe of money, its mysteriousness, its quality of not being available when you wanted it, as credit or otherwise. But outwardly he pledged loyal support.

"Whenever I hear any of these rumors that are going around, you may be sure I will contradict them," he said in parting.

But it was a feeble gesture and she knew it.

When he left the house, Dorimène could find small comfort. This talk, and what even the best members might be getting to believe, could not go on indefinitely without trouble. She was seized with a mounting anxiety, and with heavy heart turned again to the housework that she had left off.

In the quiet of her kitchen she recalled the various steps that had been taken for some years back, trying to seek reasons for what had been done. Since his illness, all her husband's leisure time had been given to the service of this idea. Well she knew his habits of reading and study, and the conversations that came out of them. As a newspaperman and later as a stenographer in the House of Commons he had come in contact with the writings of men who said the people should work together— the people, just the common people, neighbors! They should, these men said, go into little businesses together.

Their thought had gripped Alphonse deeply, she knew. The common people had never been taught to keep and control and use their own credit, he was always saying. The fruit of their thrift they were putting in the hands of others, who kept it for them, but who had the use of it all the time. The thought excited him. Always at the end of the long discussions that he had engaged in, sometimes with her, sometimes with his brother, Napoleon, he would wind up with: "One day I am determined that we will start a little bank among our people. It is what Quebec needs."

All the difficulties they had put in the way, all they could think of, had been to deter him, to put him on his guard, to save him from making a mistake. But always he had been adamant.

Though he had not gone to Europe to study what had been done there, he had corresponded with authorities whom he felt would give him guidance and the benefit of their experience. She knew, too, of the letters he had received in the preceeding years, letters encouraging him in his work, which he had carefully filed in the little desk where the bank's correspondence was kept. Seeking now every clue to restore her faith, she went to the desk and opened the file. The first letter she saw read as follows:

LONDON,
January 24, 1904

My DEAR MR. DESJARDINS:

I am truly delighted with the news in your letter of the 3rd which reaches me this morning. Ah! you will do great things in Canada and you will become known as a national benefactor. . . .

HENRY W. WOLFF

Dorimène read no further. It only added to her fears.

What did Henry Wolff of London, advocate of co-operation, know about Quebec or its people, or her people in Lévis—the volatile, gay, excitable, French Canadians who could be so easily victims of jealousy, suspicion, or emotions aroused by passionate talk? Could it be that her husband, swayed by words of praise such as the letter conveyed, was being led into a banking experiment that might end in ruin?

Her thoughts turned to Alphonse. She could see him in the House of Commons, taking down in shorthand every word that members said in debate—a patient, studious figure, bent over his desk in a central and exposed place on the floor of the Commons —so that every word uttered by the orating members could be heard and entered in the records precisely and accurately, as said, an authentic source for the French-speaking people of the Canadian democracy to find out what their elected representatives were thinking and doing in Ottawa.

The *Hansard* reporter, they called him. His shift was three hours and was called a "take." Afterward he would have to transpose his take for printing in *Hansard*.

It was a job of such responsibility that few could qualify for it. If a member were misquoted it could be a serious matter, even one of complications in the sensitive realm of party policy, ambitions, and desire to receive credit for what had been done. To Alphonse Desjardins, sitting alert and respectful, assiduously taking down the resounding and sometimes disjointed phrases of the windiest speeches as if they were gems of wisdom, came all this churned-up verbiage.

But it did not sour him. In his modesty he would speak of the great men he was privileged to hear in the House of Commons, men like Wilfred Laurier, who was showing two races the path of unity, and Henri Bourassa, the eloquent nationalist.

For his salary, Alphonse received two thousand dollars a year. On this he had to keep his house and support his family. Hardly, she thought, were they in a position to enter into a risky experiment with a bank for the people!

She sat at the little desk and wrote him. She told him of the rumors, not that they were unknown to him, but that he might be up to date. She asked him to assure her that, no matter what loss might come to the *caisse*, no charge or responsibility would be laid at their doorstep.

When his reply came, it was brief and to the point:

MY DEAR:

I have had the benefit of legal advice upon the matter of your inquiry. The caisse is not an incorporated body. The shareholders are not protected by any legal undertaking. It is really classed as a benevolent society and I, as promoter, am solely responsible. It will be so until there is a law passed that would protect such bodies. It is very necessary then to be careful with loans. But do not be alarmed at the rumors. I feel that everything will be all right.

ALPHONSE

The letter did not allay her fears. On the contrary, she was sure now that her husband didn't know where he was going.

She checked the figures for the *caisse*. There were forty thousand dollars in it. Forty thousand dollars of other people's money! They had to look after it. They got nothing for it. And if losses came through bad loans or in any other way, her husband would have to make them good.

Why, they might even lose this house! The only thing they owned!

On Wednesday afternoon Dorimène entertained at tea.

When her company had gone, Madame Parrier lingered. Madame Parrier was above all one who knew all the gossip. They were old friends. She waited in the hall until the last visiting lady had departed and came to the point:

"You may tell me, of course, that it is not my business, but everyone is talking."

"What do you mean?"

"About the *caisse populaire*."

"But why?"

"Another *caisse* has started at St. Malo."

"Alphonse told me of that some time ago." Dorimène's voice quivered and her face was flushed.

"He is, then, to be responsible for that too. What do these people know about banking?"

"It is his idea. But——"

"What folly! Dorimène, you will pardon me but I must speak frankly. Your husband is following a reckless course. Well-intentioned but reckless. Taking in money and loaning it out."

"I think I know my husband well enough to feel that he knows what he is doing," Dorimène defended stoutly, trying to suppress the tumult she felt within her.

"Banking! It is not for everyone," said Madame Parrier. "My husband! He has been a bond salesman in Montreal and he knows. It is very dangerous. You know yourself, loan money to a friend: the money it is gone; you lose the friend. In your case, where there are so many involved, why, you will lose all, Dorimène! Your whole future will be mortgaged! Surely you can persuade your husband to change his course and stop now."

Madame Parrier nodded and gestured self-righteously. She thought she was doing her good deed for the day.

Dorimène bristled, but remained politely silent.

"Believe me, it has not been easy," continued Madame. "But for the sake of the children, I would risk to speak thus to you before it is too late."

"We have always been friends, Madame Parrier."

"Yes, we have."

"Then say no more, and I will thank you for meaning well."

But when they bade good-by at the door, a coolness was between the two women.

After that Dorimène despaired of conveying her full fears to Alphonse by letter, and she knew that he could not leave his duties in Ottawa. She would do something about it; she must. Would she go to Ottawa and see him? Yes, she would take the train.

Her husband must be saved from the ruin and disgrace which she saw impending.

Chapter 2

ONE March evening when Alphonse Desjardins was only six years old his mother had said to him:

"Come, little one! Muffle up and run to the store. Bring a loaf of bread for our supper. Wait now . . ."

She went first to the baby in his cradle under the one sunny window of the little house. The baby was kicking and waving his arms, agitating to be fed.

Then she came to the mantelpiece and took down her purse. Alphonse came near, ready for his errand. When she peered into the purse he was always to remember the look that came into her face. Had she seen something shameful there?

"*Mon dieu!* the last one," he heard her breathe the words as if to herself and not for his ears. She sat down in a chair, swaying, and it was then that the blurred and wounded look got so bad in his strong mother's face that Alphonse was frightened.

But after a little he saw her take out the coin. She handed it to him. It was a five-cent piece.

"Go now, then," she said.

Alphonse ran. But the clerk scowled and flung out his arms. There was no bread in the store at that price, he said. Alphonse thought of his mother's look. He had seen it before—several times since his father had been hurt in the accident at his work and lay at home. Now he knew what it was. And he was hungry himself, too.

He hung around, uncertain. When he saw a small loaf in the

showcase his eyes stuck to it pleadingly. The odor of fresh bread and cake tantalized him. He went to the end of the counter where the clerk could see and held out his hand with the five-cent piece in it.

"I want that bread," he said in a small, determined, and reproaching voice.

"What, again! You little beggar! Shoo out of here!"

Alphonse burst into tears.

The fierce clerk was coming around the counter.

"Now get," and he stamped his foot.

When Alphonse reached the door he was crying aloud and blinded with tears. He bumped into someone. That someone, he saw when his eyes cleared, was a tall man with gray hair.

He said in English: "What's this? What's this, I say?"

"It's the stubborn kind," the clerk expostulated. "He'd make me hand over bread without the price."

"My mother sent me," Alphonse sobbed. At this the tall man came close and patted him on the shoulder and said things that Alphonse couldn't follow because he had not yet learned to speak English. But something deeper than words had already passed between them. The man went in the store and came out with a basket. In it were loaves of bread, doughnuts, and a pie.

"Start on this one," he said to Alphonse, handing him a dough-nut. "Now run home and take it all to your mother."

Alphonse ran through the dull, gathering shadows of evening. He ran fast. He was full of fear that the clerk might come running too and seize the basket.

When he got in sight of the house his two older brothers, George and Charles, came out to meet him. All was safe.

"Oh," said George, "you ate already?"

Alphonse took another bite of his doughnut.

"But yes," he said. "The basket is full. See there."

"Alphonse, where did you get such bread?" demanded Charles, his eyes popping out.

"A tall man," said Alphonse. "He gave the basket, and his talking I could not know."

"Holy Virgin," said Mother Desjardins when she heard Alphonse's story. "An *Anglais* has made us our supper this night. God reigns."

In summer the three boys roamed the river front. They watched the men at work upon the boats and ferries that came to the harbor of Lévis, their masts and sails rising above the broad St. Lawrence. These had not yet been entirely replaced by the steamboat. Lévis became known for its foundry, which supplied ships' fittings and general ironware. Foundry and shipyard gave precarious employment for the men who had their homes above the rock. Boats came from their junketings upriver and down to Gaspè and beyond to the rim of the earth. To the boys each arrival was a mysterious stranger.

Together they would watch the men at work: the builders, the ship carpenters, the fitters, the painters, the sail menders, and the hewers of the great timbers that, in the 1860's, after being formed and shaped still mostly by hand, would become part of the skeletons of the most adventuresome schooners. Lévis, though inland and situated opposite Quebec City on the bank of the St. Lawrence, had some of the ways of the sea. With sailors ofttimes in port, stopping for a time before sailing tracklessly off to far places of the earth, how could it be otherwise?

There was too much transiency for the town to get anything like the strong growth that was the birthright of Quebec across the river, where Wolfe had made his historic dash up the heights upon one September dawn—a dash which began the history of the United States of America; for on the Plains of Abraham was broken the power of France in the New World, and the Anglo-Saxons were now free to quarrel prodigiously among themselves. Over that city would continue to hover the shades of proud seigneurs; always there would be in its profile the grandeur of the first city in tradition, culture, religion, and politics of the French race in North America.

Lévis, by contrast, was the humble maidservant making her way as best she could, hewing wood and drawing water. Later she was to develop into a railway junction and see brisk spurts of employment in the building of bridges and ferries.

But in those early days she was living on the husks. Most of the families were poor, and large, as has been and is the way in French Canada; the one into which Alphonse had the fortune to be born was no exception.

Sometimes the three boys would dally so long in the morning among the workmen and along the piers that it would be noon hour and the men would be knocking off for their lunches. Then the lunch cans would be produced, and the men would sit down and munch their cold fare.

"Boys," a lank workman called out one day, laying down his broadax, "come here."

The brothers ran through the chips to him.

"One of you," said the man, "go to my house near your father's and tell my wife you are to bring back a pot of hot tea. Run now and a coin is in your hand."

All three turned and ran for the tea.

Next day the same thing happened, only more men wanted a hot dish from home.

Then and there an idea was born. The boys would carry the lunch cans.

"Here's ten cents a week for each," said the men.

"We will bring in all the meals hot," said George, speaking for the trio.

"Good, boys."

So it was.

Every day the brothers made the circuit on the dot and rushed the hot lunches to the hungry men. It was a joint project.

"Ten cents a week," said George. "There is a circus coming. I will see the elephant."

"I will buy candy," said Charles.

"Ten cents a week I will save," resolved Alphonse in silence. He was remembering the look on his mother's face the night he went for the bread.

That was all right until school opened. Then, Mother Desjardins harangued her little band. They must go to school.

Herself, she could read, but she could not write. No child of hers must be like that.

All the time that her boys were growing up she had one idea. They must go to school. No matter what it would cost her they must have education. For this purpose she was willing to deny herself anything and do any kind of work. And the death of her invalided husband did not change her determination one whit.

She could not go out to work; there was always a house and children to be taken care of. But she would have work brought in to her: she washed clothes and did ironing and mending for some well-to-do families of the town.

All this and more she did willingly that her sons might have the chance for an education. She loved her children. And clad in rough clothes, with washboard and iron, with pan and broom and brush and mop, in a round of work through the years that made her sinewed and big-armed, was this love made visible.

Though her work was hard and her hours long, there was one law that Mother Desjardins laid down and from which there was no deviation: night prayers! Each day's deeds were gathered up at night—time when the family went down on knees and communed with God. That was the teaching of Mother Desjardins. Every night she showed the living of her family to God. In her own voice, raised in the salutation of the deity, she led:

"Let us place ourselves in the presence of God and adore Him," and so on to the Rosary and prayers to good St. Anne.

That scene they would never forget from the eldest to the

youngest; even little Napoleon who was twelve years younger than Alphonse had to answer that muster call and add his small voice to the supplicating chorus.

In their mother's voice was littleness of self, adoration, pleading and a gentle tremulousness of fear, faith and hope. In the bare room of their bare house, knees to bare floor, the little brood squared off in battle with the powers of darkness and poverty, prayers blending in a symphony of human pathos.

In that squaring off, in that hour of collective reflection upon the mystery of their existence, each heard the other murmur humble and plaintive words to his Maker; compassion came into their ways, and reverence. Alphonse had grown used to it as a child. It came easy through youth and young manhood. To the end of his days the voice of the old mother at prayer would linger in his depths, to recur poignantly at the most unexpected times and places, breaking through the noises of calamity and machinery.

George, the second son, was the first to give her joy in his success.

He got on well at school. When he was sixteen, already tall and strapping, he, by adding a couple of years to his age, applied for the job of instructor at a military school. He got the job. He was good at drill. And when he came home he stood straight as a rush and was of good address.

George took pride in showing his brothers the benefits of soldierly appearance. But later he gave it up and became a reporter, and then a journalist. He married young. He took a prominent part in public affairs, and was elected to the Legislature of the Province of Quebec.

There came the great day when George Desjardins said to his mother: "I am going to make my first speech in the Legislature. I want you to be present, Mother, at the time."

"Oh, I don't know, George. It is not my place in there."

"Ah, do you not know that it is because of you that I am there today?"

"Oh, no, George, I cannot come."

"But why?"

"It is of such high class in the Green Chamber. All those notables and their wives. My clothes . . ."

"But you must have the clothes, Mother."

"They are not fashionable for a grand place like that."

"My wife will be there. And you will come, too. Please, Mother, say you will come."

"My son is a big figure. He makes laws."

"Your dresses are very nice. What do I care for style?"

She went. She and George's wife. They listened to the young orator. Very tall he was, straight and *distingué*, standing there in the forum that had heard the impassioned oratory of the leaders of French Canada from Papineau to Laurier, whose star was soon to rise in the nation.

The applause thrilled her.

Afterward George took her and his wife and introduced them to Sir Adolphe Chapleau, the Premier. The latter took her hand and said: "Madame, permit me to congratulate you. You have a son who is a very fine orator. He has proven it today."

When she came home, the others asked about the speech.

"He made a fine speech," she said. "They all said so. He is smart, that George."

When after a few days George found time to visit his mother's home, she welcomed him at the door, bowing him across the threshold as if he were some visiting dignitary, she with her sleeves rolled up.

She said gravely: "You are to be complimented, my son. Such a success as you are making already! I never did think to see the day that I would have a son in the Parliament."

George Desjardins, M.P., gripped his mother by her two big

arms. It was his way of dispelling any formality between them in his hour of success.

"See here," he cried. "It is not I who have done that. It is those two arms of yours that have put me where I am," and he shook her gently.

Now all this time, Alphonse was not standing still. Just the same, he was not going to be a quick success in the world, Mother Desjardins used to predict. He was too stubborn for one thing. He was thorough and methodical and short cuts didn't interest him.

For all of that, she would point to him as a model for the younger ones. He never stayed out at night in the beer joints or in dance halls with the girls. He was a good student, too, always at the books, especially the ones with something practical in them. Already he was teaching himself shorthand.

He was jolly, and such a good talker, and full of jokes, and so quiet that you couldn't tell he was in the house.

Ah but what an eater was that Alphonse! He never seemed to have enough.

"Alphonse has been in the pantry again," was a refrain of the Desjardins' household that held a slightly ominous note, since it was an indirect way of pointing out the disappearance of food.

Chapter 3

IT WAS not surprising that Dorimène's name was Desjardins, too, there being many of that name in the Province of Quebec. She lived in Sorel. Now and then she visited Lévis, where she stayed with her uncle, Monsieur Jean Theriault.

Alphonse did not finish college. He left after his freshman year. For a short time he went soldiering. He was a member of an expedition to Fort Garry in Manitoba, at the time of the Louis Riel rebellion, to put down the disturbance.

Alphonse learned to stand up straight, to salute and do sentinel duty. As for political views about the Riel uprising, he didn't have any at the time. This was a job, with small but regular pay —and his mother could well use the money, Alphonse thought. And that was that.

Later on, when the cause of Riel had become almost a national question, you'd not be popular in Quebec were it said you had marched against Riel on the prairie. Riel had taken the law of the region into his own hands; had arrested men and put one to death. That man happened to be a native of Ontario and a member of the Orange Order. Riel, French-Indian and said to be Roman Catholic, led successive sallies against the Canadian Government from various points in that vast territory from which new provinces were to be carved. Soon politicians began fanning the passions that underlie race and creed. Then there was hell to pay.

But well before this time Alphonse Desjardins was discharged and went home. He liked Quebec better than any place he had ever seen. His stride was firm now on the steep streets of Lévis.

A job was open on the *L'Echo de Lévis*. He took it, and worked under I. N. Belleau, who later became a judge of the Superior Court.

Later, he was on *Le Canadien*—a Quebec daily paper which had the distinction of being the first French newspaper in Canada. The paper was under Israel Tarte, a famous figure in Canadian politics, who was at the time opposed to the rising liberalism of the young lawyer, Wilfrid Laurier.

In his newspaper work Alphonse had contacts with influential people. Soon he was functioning in all the activities of a general reporter. His studious and inquiring habits of mind were great assets.

It had been on one of her visits to Lévis that Dorimène and Alphonse met. After Mass on a Sunday is a friendly moment in the Province of Quebec. Neighbor chats with neighbor, and introduces the visiting companion. It was thus that they were first introduced, under the shadow of the spire of Notre Dame de Lévis.

But it was not until he stood beside her one evening on the ferryboat from Quebec that he looked into her eyes. She was by the rail, her figure framed in the undulant motion of the river, one strand of auburn hair fluttering across her forehead. Below her heavy coat her purple dress trailed the deck. It was April, and below them on the waters of the St. Lawrence there floated a wide, white acreage of ice. The ferryboat nosed laboriously through the flux, leaving a swirl of churning water. He moved beside her and bowed.

"It does not cause one to fear, this surface ice," he said, with the assurance of a native and experienced river crosser.

"Oh, no Monsieur, the boat is quite steady."

She smiled, and he saw a mistiness in her eyes.

"Do you like to travel by boat?"

"Yes, very much. For a short way."

"I myself am a very good sailor—in sight of land," he laughed.

"It fascinates me, this," she replied. "Not the land. No, but the swirl of waters in the *sillage*." Mirth and danger blended in her voice.

His eyes followed hers to where the river surged in the wake of the boat.

"I'm so used to that, I hardly ever see it."

"You cross often, then?" she went on when he fell silent.

"Every day, to and from work on the paper."

He saw now that the mist in her eyes was surprisingly like the mist that hung above the river in summer—the River St. Lawrence, mighty and mysterious. The woman was the river made sublime.

When the boat docked they walked across the little space of level land which is the threshold of Lévis. Above them rose the naked rock, towering the space of three stories above the roof of the highest house, a gray adamant wall, its face clean and perpendicular as if cut by some giant cleaver of the gods in the makings of earth and rivers. Together they walked slowly up the winding boardwalk that pedestrians take into the town of Lévis. Here above the ledge a thousand houses were bunched upon the rolling tableland where the town has hidden its size, and much of its beauty.

Dorimène peered curiously at the houses that lined the stairway. They were bare, shabby, and full of despair. Broken windows and unhung doors gaped like the sightless eyes of the old. Some of the houses were big, ancient, and crumbling. Others were newly improvised. Some of them were but lean-to dwellings against the rock. The backyards and alleyways were sunless. The snow of winter, where it had drifted in, lay preserved by the cold and the dark to form a dirty scum oozing in the damp slope. But people were here, living here, and children in numbers.

"What a beautiful child!" remarked Dorimène, gesturing to one of three playing in a little space between the houses they were passing.

Alphonse looked toward the little girl. She had golden hair, the bluest eyes, and a bright, eager face. She did seem out of place on the ledge.

"Yes, she is a pretty one."

"She does not look at all like the others. And yet—and yet—she must belong in one of those houses."

"There are more here in this particular part than can always be accounted for," Alphonse said guardedly.

His experience as a reporter in Quebec and his daily crossings on the ferry—the river boat that carried workmen, businessmen, adventurers and adventuresses alike—left him no illusions about the nature of some of the houses that set their lamps by night under the shadows of the cliff.

"It makes one sad to see it," he went on, "when human beings fall in such case that they have to huddle in these places."

"Some of the houses are old," she said with the tact of a visitor, "but the houses above the cliff in the other part of Lévis, ah! they are very nice."

But a tenseness had seized her companion and a strong light was in his eyes.

"That rock," he said with a wide sweep of an arm, "it is clean; it is sound all through. Reliable, and the river—only a poet knows how to talk of the river! It, too, is clean and full to the brim and faithful, always there! So is the land in back. Always there and faithful to yield. Only this"—his gaze swept up and down the passage through what once could have been the rows of human habitations—"is failing. Only this is waste and tumbling."

Dorimène looked in surprise at the young man beside her. He was tall, over six feet, about twenty-four, strong and well-fleshed. There was an eager sparkle in his eyes and a genial expression about his mouth. This was not the face of a self-appointed messiah of the world. But now there was turbulence and determination.

"You feel deeply about such things," she said.

"There is not only this," he said. "There is also the experience
of my mother. How she worked and slaved that we might have
bread—and education! Our father was an invalid a long time
before he died."

"When it comes like that it can be so very deep," she added in
tones slow and compassionate.

"It is my dream to do something about it some day," he went
on. "Something that would help the people of our race in their
needs. I am not bitter, but . . ."

Almost instinctively she moved close to his side. Her eyes
looked up at him with more than admiration.

"It is of your writing that you speak?"

"Some day I hope to own a newspaper of my own. There are
things that I will want to say for our people."

They had reached by now the top of the cliff and turned. For
a moment the grandeur of this breath-taking view of the broad
St. Lawrence swept the undertow of squalor from their minds.

Only a poet could speak of the river, as Alphonse said. It was
something you felt, a presence, silent and serene. It had an arcane
vitality of its own, collected from the far-outstretched limbs of
the continent. For a moment, as Dorimène gazed, its motion
seemed to be in reverse—the vast surface of its floating ice field
moving upstream—and it mystified her until Alphonse explained.
The ocean tides hundreds of miles east come this far into the St.
Lawrence and influence the flow of the waters at times.

Across was Quebec. Standing at the top of the ledge, they
could see the other half of the riven, huge bulk of rock that stands
under the Plains of Abraham. In the gathering twilight they
could see roofs and spires and the broad spread of clustered,
ancient homes.

Valiant deeds spoke in a hundred monuments and history whispered through the roofs and gestured serenely in stone. It was a
city at which they looked with their eyes. But what their French
blood told them was the story of their race—its struggle, its ter-

rain, its culture—of which Quebec is the mother. Rock and river and race!

As Dorimène and Alphonse walked in the streets of Lévis, they found within them exultation.

It was the beginning. When her stay in Lévis was over and she went back to Sorel, he was a visitor at her home there. And later, when she came more often to Lévis, his calls at her uncle's home were regular.

If courtship is the school of gallantry, the Quebec environment took nothing from that. The long, cold winters, instead of being an impediment, were rather the opposite, furnishing many occasions for the companionship of two. Horses and sleighs didn't require anything like the investment of the modern automobile. Alphonse turned out to salute his lady behind a sleek, beribboned charger, chafing at the bit, with jingling bells and warm buffalo robes and snowy roads beckoning. Then skating and skiing parties were no less carnivals of fun and gaiety.

When old winter makes its first passes at the region there are many skirmishes and blustering storms, then the big cold comes in and the regime steadies down. For two weeks without a break the thermometer will have registered twenty degrees below zero every night, relenting only to eight above by high noon. All this time the ground is white. There is brilliant dryness in the air. In the mornings a haze hangs on the low places and trails upward toward the distant hills. Toward noon the sun has warmed the earth and the face can stand the biting air. Mostly it is calm, a still cold in comparison with the coastal region.

The days are bright and the children are full of pep, racing with sleds and skates and sticks and skis, tumbling and rolling themselves in the snow. By late afternoon there is a clatter in the outdoor rinks; you hear the scrape of skates along the ice, then the noise of sticks, pucks shot to the boards, and cry of eager young voices at play. It is the same in all the villages.

In a few hours the weather has changed. Warm currents of air have moved in from somewhere. The temperature goes up about twenty-five degrees. That is the time. On the evening of such a day the sting has gone from the air and in indescribable mellowness hangs close to earth. The antiseptic frost has done something.

For the two lovers it was a double joy to walk on such nights, breathing the medicated air; it was like wine, sweet and exhilarating.

He had never loved any woman, and no woman had ever loved him. Dormène had never loved any man. The newness of possessing another and of being in turn possessed amazed and exalted them.

Hitherto, in the years of their growing up, had been bafflement and frustration, patience and endurances and waiting upon the happiness of others.

Now, at the threshold of youth, the walls of life had opened. There, spread prodigally before them, was an endowment of riches. The tides of being were coming in.

Now no hope was too high; no height was unassailable. Compared to what had already happened, all else would be trivial. They were in young love.

"Isn't it a long day for you?" she asked softly, smiling into his eyes. "I thought the ferry would never get in."

"Do you watch that close?"

"Oh, I can hear the toot."

"As for the work I do, it is very interesting. Even exciting, Dorimène."

"You mean the questions you are writing about? I read the papers every day, you know."

"Well, that, and the people you meet."

"I'm afraid," she said, and her voice faltered, "that you will be working too hard."

She moved closer to him. They walked with muted stride; he could feel her shiver against him.

"Afraid?" he laughed. "When I face homeward on the river and think of you, Dorimène, that word has no meaning." His voice was deep and strong.

She straightened, then swayed and tossed her auburn hair; her eyes became tender with affection.

"Alphonse, does your family know? Know about us?"

"Oh, yes; my mother thinks you're most sweet. And every good Frenchwoman expects her sons to marry. And on your side, Dorimène?"

"Oh, Uncle Johnny Theriault? Yes, he thinks you are the one. A fine character, he says, and very good-looking."

They walked slowly, savoring a happiness that had suddenly made of creation something special for them alone.

They strolled to the town's outskirts and turned homeward.

All around the vast pervading whiteness, the snow made the ground more level than it really was. From clear depths overhead the stars shone down like blue steel points. On this clean, winter-made terrain, life leaped within the young and rejoiced. The moonbeams danced upon the ski runs; mirthful voices arose from the rinks and ponds and sleighs. All around was laughter in the night.

"Isn't it lovely! Out at a time like this!" she exulted in her low, rich voice.

Alphonse paused before he could say what he wanted.

"There is no loveliness like having you close, Dorimène." He put his arm clumsily around her shoulders.

"Don't, don't, Alphonse," she pleaded, squirming out of his reach. But she had already caressed him with her tones.

And they fell reverently silent at their discovery.

Uncle Johnny was not disturbed when Alphonse came and sat with Dorimène in the parlor at night. He had been observing carefully the young Desjardins these many months. One brother was a member of Parliament, too, already.

All was being well conducted, he felt sure. Alphonse never kept the girl up too late. This was an important point with Uncle

Johnny. Come eleven o'clock, he claimed, it was "time for all honest men to be in their beds and dogs on the road." This was a proverb.

In case a suitor did stay too late, there was the well-known institution of the clock-winding. The big old-fashioned clock stood in the corner. At the deadline Uncle Johnny would enter. There would be a polite and formal inventory of the current defaults in the weather, a prophecy of further perversity on its part, and a throat-clearing or two. Then Uncle would turn his attention to the clock. It had to be wound on two sides. If the visitor made no move there would be a pause filled with interrogation after the first winding. When the second winding was finished the solemn rite was over. No yawn need now be stifled, the fleetingness of time having been established beyond all doubt.

One night Uncle Johnny had just finished winding one side. There came a knock at the door. Uncle Johnny went out.

Alphonse had risen to leave. Suddenly the impulse seized him.

"Dorimène, will you marry me?"

"You know I will, Alphonse."

They stood and kissed while the old clock ticked off the seconds.

Uncle Johnny's footsteps sounded returning in the hall. It was only a neighbor lady who had come to borrow a cup of sugar for the morrow's breakfast.

"Then set the date; set the date," whispered Alphonse. "I know a small place we can get to live in until we can build a house of our own."

They married that same year of 1879.

Chapter 4

ALPHONSE had been determined to master shorthand. It was, he considered, a necessary part of a reporter's qualifications—an idea that was held more in those days than in recent years. In his studious way he had found time to keep at it tenaciously. Between assignments, while waiting for a galley to come out from the composing room to be proofread, during his nights off, he assiduously studied and practiced this art.

At that time a certain need was being felt in the Legislature of the Province of Quebec. It was that a more complete and accurate record should be kept of the various debates that took place in the Chamber. Alphonse's newspaper experience had given him some knowledge of political affairs and he had friends in the Legislature. With his ability at shorthand, he soon had the qualifications of a court stenographer. He felt sure that he could get this contract and publish the debates.

He told Dorimène the idea he had in mind.

"I would be there at the sessions of the Legislature and take down everything that was said in debate."

"That will be very hard, I should think," she said.

"It will be a stenographic report."

"And for what purpose?"

"To have the record—an official record and printed."

"Oh, something that could be looked back to in case of dispute. I see."

"Yes, and not only that. Sometimes when a member stands up

and talks plain for what his constituency wants, he likes to have what he said written down somewhere so his followers can read it."

"Sort of getting the message back home."

"That's it."

"But wouldn't it work the other way, too?"

"How do you mean?"

"Well, suppose a member took a stand on some big question," Dorimène had a note of warning in her voice, "and then later he changes his mind—or perhaps the stand he took becomes unpopular?"

"It is possible, that, what you foresee," Alphonse admitted.

"In such a case it wouldn't be to his advantage to have what he said on the record. His enemies could make use of that." Dorimène was searching out the weak points.

"And then you mean they might try to have the business stopped?"

"After a few experiences, yes."

"Just the same there is the need for the record. After all we speak of representative government. And how are the people to know—if the record is not kept?"

"There is then the other side to be considered," Dorimène's face brightened. "If, for example, a member debated in the Legislature on a point that became an important issue and on the side that the people desired, he would be pleased to have his words on the record."

"Exactly, Dorimène," he said. "You know, you think of everything. I never saw the like of you." His gay eyes thrilled. He ran his hands through his thick shock of hair, like a man preparing himself with zest for work ahead.

"I'm glad of that, Alphonse. Glad you think there's no one like me." Their glances met and held.

In a little while she said: "You speak of representative government, and that the people should know what their leaders are thinking and doing. Very good. But what will you and I get out of this, Alphonse?"

His brow puckered. For a moment he had no reply.

"I can have them printed quite economically," he said. "I can sell some. Then, I count on the government buying enough to make it worth my while."

"Alphonse, is it at your own risk you are undertaking this?"

He fell silent.

"At my own risk and peril," he replied after a little.

"Ah, it is of the good of the people you are thinking. As I said, with you it is like a devotion, that. But do you forget there is also us? There are our children that are coming, Alphonse."

"In this work there must also be a livelihood," he defended.

"And you know we can't go on living here," Dorimène continued. "No space. With a family we'd be under each other's feet."

"We will build a house of our own," Alphonse assured her. We have been saving for that. Wait a little. You will see."

Her face lit up.

"Ah, Alphonse, how happy we will be in our own house! When you are away all day at work in Quebec how glad I'll be to fix up our own home. That will be living. Here in a little rented space, what's the use . . ."

He smiled at her—at her whom he called the much-loved companion of his life—enjoying already the zeal of her home-building and companionship.

And so it was.

Alphonse Desjardins became the publisher of the debates of the Legislature of the Province of Quebec. It was a full-time job. He listened to the debates and took them down verbatim. These he later transcribed and printed at his own risk and cost. He was not an official employee but had the job on a contract.

At the end of the first year the government bought 400 copies at ten dollars each. It was enough to enable him to go on. He received no salary.

It was the rule to submit galley proof to the members. They might make minor changes, but could not change the meaning of the speeches they had made.

His office, though that of a modest clerk, was also one of public trust—as was later to be proven. It had the advantage of giving him close knowledge of what was going on in political circles, contacts with the men who were making the politics of Quebec, and an insight into the processes by which legislation is brought in and passed—a fund of experience that was to stand him in good stead in his later struggles.

It was laborious, exacting, and responsible work. He had, of course, to be present at all sessions in the Green Chamber and take down the rapid-fire debate of members whose natural speed of talk was often accelerated by political passion. It is easy to think that not everyone wanted to be put on the record in such contests of verbal righteousness—contests which through the reporter's initiative could be relayed and placed before the eye of the electorate.

As in the case with every man who settles down, his life now became divided between his work and his home. While the House was in session, Dorimène always wanted to know what was going on in the debates, sharing Alphonse's respect for the best men in public life.

Sometimes they would talk of the questions that then were to the fore in Quebec—for the Green Chamber was and is more than a legislature in the ordinary provincial sense; it is also the forum of a culture and a race. The early years of their married life went swiftly. Children were born to them. And, more insistent than at first, their thoughts would turn to a house of their own with clean space and light and air and room to live.

Chapter 5

ALPHONSE made long strides up the cliff. This evening he hurried straight from the boat to tell her. The shadows gathered in and over his shoulder and the lights of Quebec came on and the shapes of ferries moved more cautiously on the silent river. That day he had put through the bargain for a building lot.

He was still half-winded when Dorimène let him in.

"Good news," he said. "We've got the lot."

"Ah, bravo!" Dorimène was elated.

"Is it on that same location you said?"

"Yes, corner of Guenette and Blanchet."

"About there? Tell me more."

"A quiet street. And close enough to the ferry and everything," he said.

"Guenette! Why, yes. It is quite residential, and runs toward the cliff. I know."

"Our house will be almost in front of Notre Dame de Lévis on the opposite side."

"Right there? What a spot, Alphonse!"

"And what a view!" he told her. "High above the river and Quebec beyond.

"It will be, besides, close to the College of Lévis where your friends are," she went on.

"Right, and it's clean, not packed, and free of noise, too," he added.

"And will there be business places near—like stores and a

bakery?" Dorimène asked, her housekeeping instincts coming to the surface after the first flurry of elation over where their future home was to be.

"Near enough—well, convenient, but not too near."

And they fell to work on the plan of the house, putting their heads together above the kitchen table even before they have finished their supper.

Alphonse lit his pipe. He had several, and was a heavy smoker. An hour passed. On bits of paper they outlined the kind of house they wanted—basement, kitchen, upstairs and down.

"And that dormer upstairs will be facing the river, and a little balcony here could be put where anyone could stand and get the view of the St. Lawrence," Alphonse was filling in the rough sketch.

Suddenly Dorimène's face grew serious.

"Alphonse, you haven't eaten."

He looked up from the sketches.

"You haven't touched your food."

"It must be the excitement," he jollied her.

"It is not the first time you have not eaten. Two evenings last week—yes, two times," she recounted now with anxiety.

Alphonse shrugged it off and looked disinterestedly at the food. But she was troubled.

In the next year the house-building filled their thoughts and spare time. They learned through experience the value of thrift, and saw how an unguarded borrower might fall into the clutches of the moneylenders. Alphonse knew his position was better than that of the majority. He was publisher of the debates of the Legislature, a position of public trust and held in high respect by his fellow citizens. He rubbed elbows every day with the most influential men in the province. If he found it hard to establish a roof of his own, what must be the plight of the unbefriended little citizen with nothing but his two hands and his willing-to-be-honest character when money, if it could be borrowed at all, often had to be paid for at very high rates of interest?

At last the plans for building the house were ready and the job was given to a contractor. This man, however, failed to come through with the required results in time, and at one stage of construction the work had to be taken over by Aphonse himself.

In some of the carpentry he was helped by his younger brother Napoleon, who cut a sliver from his left thumb, leaving a mark which he bore the rest of his life.

The house they built was, somehow, not like any other house in Lévis. It was not ornate but it had a certain distinction. It was spacious, with an L built to the rear. The house had nine rooms and stood high above the cliff, commanding a view of the river and Quebec beyond. There was grace in the high dormer and the little balcony that faced the river. The view of the house seen by one coming along Guenette was one of good lines and proportion.

To the right at some distance there loomed the stone walls of the College of Lévis and the Seminary. Still closer was the beautiful old stone Church of Notre Dame de Lévis, its interior done in gold colors. During Holy Week it was draped in purple and black, with the aged men and women of the neighborhood coming in at all hours to recite their Aves.

If you opened the left door of that church coming out, the first house you would see was the house that Alphonse Desjardins built. It was a gracious, human dwelling with elbowroom and clean space. It was quiet there, quiet enough to let a thought go deep if it wanted to. And the chimes from yonder steeple reverently reported the passing of the hours. At this hearth, while their own children were being born, Alphonse Desjardins could dream and plan and study.

The decade from 1880 to 1890 was a stirring time in Canadian politics. The union of the provinces had come in 1867—in principle and in legislation. But the spirit of unity, and actual unity, had still to come. Wilfrid Laurier's own paper had said that Quebec didn't care a fig for the English-speaking provinces. That was in his early days before he came, a dark horse from the Athabaska polls, a lone Liberal elected when the other constituencies sent in a Conservative landslide.

Laurier's talents were shown to be such that he did not stay long in Quebec. His first speech brought acclaim. He was soon called to Ottawa as a member of the Dominion Parliament. His sincerity, eloquence, and understanding won all. Instead of being an enemy of confederation and unity he now became its shining advocate.

In Quebec the political pot boiled fiercely. Men took public questions seriously, and one cause after another agitated them. There were the question of the Jesuit estates, the Louis Riel rebellion in the Northwest with its underpull of racial passion, the separate-school question, the relations between the provinces and the Dominion.

Last but not least there were the scandals, in railways and contracting and the use of public funds, which fell on both of the great parties at the beginning of the nineties. This was the time that Israel Tarte, publisher of *Le Canadien*, on which Alphonse Desjardins had formerly worked, left his former political friends and joined forces with Wilfrid Laurier.

It all gave sharp pitch to political feeling at Quebec. Laurier's meteoric rise had given the French a new interest in politics. There were now not only the local sphere but the Dominion as well. The game of factionalism was on. The air was tense.

Chapter 6

ONE evening Alphonse came late from the Chamber to his home. He started to tell Dorimène about the heated debates that had taken place among the members that day.

She liked to hear these episodes described; for not only were her ideas of public questions acute, but to hear him gave her an insight into his work and responsibilities in the long, arduous sessions.

He had only just started when his voice trailed off into incoherent syllables. She went to him. He had fallen asleep exhausted on the couch. His face, she saw, had become drawn and haggard. His wrist that had fallen across his chest attracted her attention. It was its color. It seemed yellowish.

He slept soundly—the dead sleep of exhaustion.

What would they do if anything happened to him?

The next day she put it to him.

"You must see a doctor, Alphonse."

He was dressing himself wearily, preparing for work.

There was no answer.

"You need a rest. You must knock off!"

He was keeping his head down—as if he could not face her. She poured his coffee and buttered his toast. He would have to face her at the eating.

He came to the table with his hat on. He looked at her and said slowly: "Dorimène, I've been to the doctor. I didn't want to tell you——"

"What did he say?" She stood up.

"He didn't say. He can't say. Doesn't seem to know."

She breathed a sigh of relief.

"Well, it could be worse. It could be something so definite that he could tell."

He smiled wanly.

"Sometimes I wish I did know—the worst," he said grimly.

"It is a year since you have shown a steady appetite, Alphonse; you who used to be a big eater."

"Dorimène," he said, "You must not worry."

"Eat," she pleaded, "eat." She went to the pantry to get a bit of the jam he liked best.

When she came back, he had gone. The meal on the table was untouched.

When Alphonse reached his office in the Parliament Building it was to give his attention to a complicated incident that had been dragging on for quite some time but had come to a point on the preceding day.

It was the spring of 1889. In a few days the session would adjourn for the year. Previously a Very Important Political Personage had made a statement in the Green Chamber. Alphonse had taken it down in his notebook. This statement concerned a Conference on Dominion Provincial Relations which had been invited to sit in Quebec. According to the statement Quebec would not have to bear any of the costs. This was later found impossible. In a short time the opposition had gotten busy on the implications of the statement, and it soon became clear that the prestige and popularity of the Important Political Personage might suffer before the eyes of the electorate. When debate ensued over what had been said he denied that that was what he meant. A squabble was on. The air got thick. Members gestured strenuously, carving the air magnificently with their hands.

At such a time oratory becomes much more than a use of words. It becomes a craft employing especially the hands but really all the body in gesticulation, squirming, and stamping. The man who has the floor will yank an idea from below his knees, draw it gradually breast-high, where he hugs it for a while, then to his lips, where he shapes it lovingly, to send it finally flaming from his forehead. In this spirited manual dialectic there lives on something of the fencing-master style and swordsmanship of France of the Foundation of Quebec.

When calmness came and settled down all eyes were turned to Alphonse.

"What will be in the official record?"

Alphonse spent a long time looking back through his notes. Shortly, adjournment was called for the day, and most of the members busied themselves with other matters.

The next morning, Alphonse had no sooner sat down in his office when there presented himself an under boss whose special role seemed to be to ride herd on strays or other persons who might, either by truth or error, cause embarrassment to the party.

Alphonse was not a party man. In the debates all were treated alike. The under boss swaggered. He stuck thumbs in his vest. He stuck out a heavy belly. He expressed a strong desire to read and edit a certain passage in the debates before the issue went to press. Alphonse refused.

"What, then, is going to appear in the printed issue?" asked the Belly.

"It was taken down as was said," Alphonse replied.

"But it was not said—in that sense—not meant——"

"I cannot take the liberty of changing the meaning of a statement," Alphonse protested.

"Make no mistake, my good man. This must not go out in the printed debates to be read by the people. If the opposition is mean enough to make a dirty mess out of this . . ." The Belly by now had a glare in his eye and was walking up and down in front of Alphonse's desk.

"But, sir, do you realize what you are asking?" Alphonse said.

"I am not given my office to change what members say in the Chamber but to record it."

"It seems, Monsieur Desjardins, that you have become very finicky. Very finicky!"

Alphonse ignored the taunt.

"There is not only myself. Other members heard what was said. If I should change that in the printed issue what faith would anyone have in the public records?"

"Oh, my word, this is a most delicate conscience that you are exhibiting, Monsieur Desjardins."

"What can I do? I tell you, even were I willing to make such a change, there would be the others."

"The others! Pouf! It is of them you are thinking. Well, let them forget."

"And even if they would—what of the ethics of my position?"

"And there it goes," snorted the Belly. "A regular damned fly-trap of a conscience."

Alphonse reddened and then paled.

"And too delicate, I'm afraid, to be durable," went on the Belly with hauteur. A cold, cynical curl was gathering in the lower corners of his mouth.

"A man has a contract to print the *Debates*. That may be ended by this Legislature. He should have the sense to make his conduct agreeable. I would be sorry for you—if you were not such a fool." It was the parting shot. He turned to go, but wheeled:

"Once more. Will the wording be changed?"

Alphonse took off his glasses. He looked up at the man from his desk. Their glances were charged, as if something obscene were being discussed. He lowered his head and shook it from side to side. Now his stubbornness seized him suddenly and he said: "No. It cannot be tampered with, I tell you." And in a voice that could be heard through the corridors he roared: "Get out!"

When the under boss had gone, Alphonse stared vacantly at the boards in the floor. The threat was not lost upon him. His stare

was the stare of a man who is insulating himself for a moment
from the guile of his kind, gathering his forces. His body writhed
in the chair—the reaction of an organism that finds poisons gen-
erating within it.

He stared long. He was seeing in the chambers of his mind the
jungle ways of politics: The truth is often betrayed by that leader
who feels he must keep his grip *at any price*. In this case it was as
much the fault of the opposition, which was trying to make as
much as it could out of a statement that had been given without
thought.

Clearly, the democratic process has to be redeemed from its
own internal secretions. It had to be purged, cleansed, and re-
baptized by forces other than itself.

As to the way that these debates should be printed, Alphonse
had a clear idea of his own. Why, he had written it down already.
He pulled himself to his feet, crossed the floor to where the back
files of the *Debates* were stacked, and turned up the statement
that he had written:

The present volume completes the first period of ten years of the
existence of the *Debates*. Ten years! It is in every way a career for
our Canadian publications of a particular character such as this.
Founded in 1879, with the firm determination to make their way and
to live whatever happens, with the understanding of their usefulness
being admitted, the *Debates* have fought all obstacles with courage
and perseverance.

The beginnings have been stormy and full of trouble. The sympathetic encouragement of public men, of whatever political shade,
as well as the help, always so generous which my fellow members
of the press have never ceased to grant me, here is the secret of these
ten years of laborious existence.

Though short be this period, much precious material, however, has
been accumulated for the history of our dear province! The *Debates*,
with their fourteen thousand pages of parliamentary speeches, are
happy to say that they will supply a large share of the information
to the historian who will search for the causes of the events of which
we have been the witnesses.

To all those who have been willing to help me in a venture so new,
for the efforts of a single person, and so difficult to carry out success-

fully, to the press, French and English, I offer my sincere feelings of gratefulness on the closing of this first period of ten years. May they permit me to express the hope that their precious concurrences will not fail me in the future.

I deeply solicit the sympathies of all, experience having shown to me that they are a powerful motive of encouragement in the performance of so considerable a work.

The rules of the strictest impartiality will continue to be scrupulously observed in the future as in the past. The *Debates* record which is being spoken within the legislative walls, but they have no preference for any one. This is their main merit and for no consideration whatever would they consent to change a line of conduct which alone can assure their existence.

There it was! Yes, and there below it was the name, Alphonse Desjardins. He'd stick to it. Fourteen thousand pages of orations taken down. God be praised! He'd stick to it; let them think what they like.

When, after some time, the current edition of the *Debates* came out, the members' eyes popped. There in cold type was the contested statement, printed without doctoring.

The fat was in the fire.

An Important Political Personage had been rebuffed.

Alphonse lost out. It took the official wrath a little while to catch up with him, but catch up it did. It soon became clear that at the end of the year his contract to print the *Debates Desjardins*, as they had come to be called, could not be renewed. Things were made too disagreeable for him. It amounted to this that he was frozen out.

The blow of this was bunted somewhat by his fear of his health. Yet he established and edited a daily newspaper, *L'Union Canadienne*. Editorially it was marked by dignity, frankness, and vigor. He espoused self-help, home rule, a sane nationalism; but he scotched the people who would incite race against race and creed against creed for their own political ends. Unfortunately, it only lasted about three months.

He was, by this time, a man shrunk in his clothes. His face was haggard and his friends were beginning to think that his hold on life was uncertain.

He fought it on his feet as long as he could but at last his doctor ordered him to bed.

He had served eleven years as publisher of the *Debates* in Quebec.

Chapter 7

During the first days that he had to spend in bed a vague fear pursued him. It was always there, lurking in his subconscious—but it was the worst at night.

It was then it crouched at every passageway from mind to under mind, using its various disguises and doubles to stalk him in his dreams. When fully awake he knew it for what it was: the Fear of his yet undiagnosed illness.

Though nameless it had voices: it taunted him—and he tried to answer it back point by point.

"I am your nameless malady. Good to be nameless. I might be this. Or that. Or worse. You can't tell what I might turn out to be. . . ."

And his conscious mind would think in reply:

"The doctor will find out what I have."

"It is one thing to find out what a man has—another thing to cure it."

It was in that twilight zone between real sleep and full wakefulness that the Fear worked hardest. His mind was then disarmed of its rational powers, and the impulses that were repressed to the subconscious came out and ran riot in the realm of feeling. Despair came heavy and hit his heart dead plumb at such a time. Men die at four o'clock in the morning.

Dorimène, though saddened by Alphonse's illness and the loss of his job—their sole means of livelihood—did not give in to her fears. Through the early years of their married life she had always been full of helpfulness. She now became a veritable fortress of good cheer. She cared for him lovingly day and night and was always seeking to tempt his appetite with her choicest home cooking.

The children likewise she rallied to assist on the side of health and optimism, sending them to his room with gifts and on errands of cheer. Raoul, the oldest, was then nine. Alphonse so loved his children that he was moved to tears at the thought of any harm coming to them. Thus to have them near him and to note their tender helplessness and trustfulness only added to his burden, at times filling him with a sense of his own default. He had almost a sense of guilt, lying on his back experiencing weakness and nausea, while the little ones played and scampered and shrieked about the house blissfully unaware that their breadwinner was down.

Dorimène was discreet about the visitors she would let in to see him. Those who she knew would only annoy him she put off with the word that he was to rest for a few days. But her good and jolly friend, Solomon Therrien, the cobbler, she let in, hoping that he might cheer up Alphonse with his jokes and gossip. Solomon was a shoe repairer who claimed he read the future of his clients from the way they wore the soles of their shoes, just as some clairvoyant ladies read teacups.

"It is not to mislead you with an expression of sorrow that I come," said Solomon. "I tell anyone who enquires at the shop, 'a man who wears as even an instep as Alphonse Desjardins has nothing to fear of the future.'"

Solomen beamed his friendliest smile, his wide lips flexible and almost corrugated from the long holding of tacks as his nimble fingers fitted them under the stroke of his hammer.

"If only the doctor," said Alphonse, "could read the future in my stomach as easily as you do in my shoes!" Nevertheless there was no irritation in his voice and he tried to smile at his friend.

"And as for the heels! Well, there is not a member of the society of Artisans of Lévis that shows a straighter stride."

"But you cannot say what might be done when the shoes are off."

"Anyhow, they know in Quebec that you do not go pussy-footing in your stocking feet when it comes to politics."

There was no answer.

Solomon's efforts to cheer Alphonse seemed in vain and he fell back on the platitudes of the sickroom: "You will be well and strong again soon."

Inwardly Alphonse thought: "I had health once. Now I haven't. What proof have I that it will come back?"

Outwardly he said: "Oh, yes, I think so."

"You've been working hard," went on Solomon. "A little rest now will do you good." He was getting ready to go.

"There's nothing like lying in bed to bring on worry and un-happiness," thought Alphonse. Aloud he said: "Nothing like lying in bed to make a man think."

"Yes," said Solomon in the voice of an amateur, "the mind gets rested and thinks well."

"Why doesn't he go?" thought Alphonse.

"You know, I wouldn't mind a week off myself," said Solomon. "Carving soles and driving tacks. All the same every day."

"He'll be here all night," thought Alphonse. He found it hard to talk from the pillow, lying on his back. It was pushing the words upward with your jaws.

"Your health is good always?" said Alphonse raising a faint concern in his voice.

It was unfortunately the signal Solomon needed.

"Never in twenty years have I had an ache or a pain," he went on, launching into an account of his good health and all the beer he could drink, apparently with nothing but beneficial con-sequences.

"It's queer justice," thought Alphonse. "Some have less health than is good for them. Others have more health than is good for them. Others have none."

He was rescued by Dorimène, who tactfully conveyed to the shoemaker that her patient must rest.

Alphonse always awoke now to one voice: the Fear telling him that he was an invalid.

It was the time of the utmost mental anguish. Not that the Fear let him alone at all through the day as he tried to pass the time in bed.

Who shall chart the feelings of a human being, step by step, as illness invades the body? First come the subtle warnings and indefinable malaise. Bit by bit they add up, with the victim trying to refute and explain each occasion away. Then recurrence demolishes the mental defenses and binds in a new chain of fear. Something clutches at the heart as the body musters its forces darkly against the foe. Bitterly mounts the evidence that this is a house of mortal clay indeed. Anguish of mind exceeds the suffering of the body.

Here he was after his years of struggle. Married and with five children to support. He was out of work. Not only that, he was sick in bed in a room in the house they had built.

What was it all about?

He felt like a fool stretched between the sheets, and kicked at the bedclothes, so that Dorimène was always straightening them out. The flowers she put on his table irked him. They were a symbol of sickness. He, the breadwinner, was lying now all day between sheets; he who had been so stout and strong and proud of his physique and such a good eater all his life.

As for food, the very thought of it was repulsive. His stomach suffered constantly.

Equally as much as physical pain and weakness, the question of the why of the affliction tormented him. He experienced all the natural rebellion and humiliation of the strong man who becomes seriously ill for the first time.

In him, as in all the strong under attack, there was taking place the battle of the two strengths: the blood of youth quick in power of health, and disease with a secret power of its own dark nature. In the very old and worn out the battle is tepid: in the young it is fierce and deadly. Alphonse's mind stood an awe-stricken spectator to this drama within himself. If the mind took too avidly to recovery, if it put its all on the fate of the body, it itself risked defeat and even destruction in case of the body's failure. Yet his mind must keep up the body with hope. But the outcome of the battle of the two strengths was uncertain—and he was thus plunged into a cruel dilemma, his mind not knowing where its habitation was to be, nor what world to give its attention to.

Thus is a man split in two by affliction.

It was on this state that Alphonse came to meditate. Questions seemed bright to him that he had never thought of before, and deep soundings took place. That something within him that expected to survive all, which he could only think was his soul, now threatened with eviction by the failings of the body, began to eye itself.

Thus, when Dorimène tried to convey to him some of her own abounding cheerfulness, giving him the small news of the town and the light bits of gossip of the street, he remained unresponsive. Alphonse was fascinated with the question, "What part of me, then, is the true I?"

He would feel embarrassed to say it in so many words out loud.

"The body? It cannot be: it is not the same body as when I was a child. The body has even changed completely every seven years, they say. The body may be dead in a month—or a year."

"When you can see your body going down under your very nose you know you are not it entirely."

Beyond it was something. He knew that before—vaguely by faith.

Alphonse appeared to stare straight up at the ceiling. He saw it not. He was experiencing that state of abstraction in which the invalid—every invalid—explores in loneliness the mysteriousness of existence.

There were interludes. He could hear downstairs the entry of the doctor. A rapping—a door opening and shutting—an exchange of quiet voices. Then his doctor bustling up the stairs bag in hand.

How reliable are the ears—when so much depended.

The doctor took the pulse and temperature. He hung his stethoscope to his ears and listened to heart and lungs. He kneaded Alphonse's abdomen gently in search of inflammation.

He was baffled.

He left powders that were supposed to settle a stomach, and a tonic of wild cherry. Rest in bed, he prescribed, would do wonders. In the meantime he would have the case under close observation.

All very good!

But what Alphonse really thought was, "Why should I be here at all?"

He felt that he could say he had been doing the best he knew by his wife and family, by his job, by his country and his Church and his God. And here he was knocked out flat.

He was tempted to be more angry with his God than with his doctor.

The poor doctor! What could he do?

The human body was a mystery, too, and only gave up any of the secrets of its ways grudgingly. God was the author of that. God had made the body of man out of the slime of the earth, as the Bible said. By what process he had done that, and how long it took, no one knew. But the secrets of the body's functioning were so well locked in that when a disorder came no one could guarantee it being set right; and as for life itself no man knew what it was.

Alphonse went back to staring straight up at the ceiling.

He was seeing now not with the eyes but with the all of him. Funny he'd never thought of that before. His senses, his memory, his reason and whatever else it was in a man that sat still in judgment over him, he was seeing with them all as greater eyes.

That of him which saw this was the soul, he could believe.

The soul was the essential I.

Seeing with this whole vision, he came to tap an inner realm of conviction. There was the divine in us and it outlasted disease and death.

But his mind would fall quickly from this height and he would grovel in anxiety about the cares of the present.

How long he might be sick he could not know. Given health he would get another job. His experience and his competence would guarantee that. But if the illness lasted, how could they get along in between!

Who would pay the bills?

Where could money be borrowed in such a case?

One did not wish to embarrass one's friends, and so went to a loan company. There was one man who had done that. He borrowed twenty dollars only. He paid one dollar a month interest on it. This he kept up for thirty months. Thirty dollars. Then he was sued for the original twenty dollars.

What could the poor do?

The poor! On Sundays they came together and heard the Word of God. They knelt and bowed and spoke to their Maker—some with fervor, others just going through the lines. They looked up toward an altar, trying to feel awed at the God Who was there. They were preached at and exhorted to. But who saw their pain on Monday, Tuesday, Wednesday, Thursday, Friday, and Saturday? Was God's love something bottled up for Sunday and dated on the other days? Who knew their hunger? Who could stop to reflect that a thousand needles of anxiety were stabbing at their consciousness; that shoes were worn through, that children's clothes were torn, that rain was furrowing down the shingles of the roof and the wind was blowing them off; that cold rushed in under blankets at night and made bodies shiver; that disease lurked at every turn; that age came on, inevitable; that the fang of pain was so feared by all men that it put a screen between the one who had it and his kind; that the memory of all a man had suffered in the past could well up suddenly within him and strike him down, bitter with despair; that if nature marshaled her forces to make and supply man, she was as actively engaged in destroying him; and that at times all existence bit and chewed at his nerve ends? We were promised merit in Heaven, if we suffered patiently in this life. He couldn't make it sink in. And, anyhow, by what were the pains suffered by a human being measured? By what means, on what tablet, were they recorded?

Must a man bear in silence so long that he would sink so far that he would never get back?

He remembered the case of LeSarre, a man who had committed suicide in the city, when he was on *Le Canadien*. They began poking into his affairs then, the people of the neighborhood, led by one kind old lady (who had a good nose for tragedy). They found he had been living in extreme poverty, illness, and neglect for years.

Who knows how many times he tried to get across to someone that he needed help? And failed?

Was it, then, the indifference of others that was also a crime? Was indifference the worst kind of hate? If you hate a man actively and go out and strike him, there is a commotion; and, whatever it is, it is out in the open and he may get redress, even be a hero. But if you simply ignore a man in his suffering—even as the working masses were ignored in some countries that called themselves Christian—what then!

Yes, in a way this is true: There's a slimy silence in indifference that makes it worse than hate.

There was One who said: "I will have you hot or cold, but the lukewarm I begin to vomit out of my mouth."

How would anyone understand? In the cities and in the villages too were many people like LeSarre, living in attics and cabins, men and women unutterably lonely, separated from human understanding by an affliction or a psychological trait. It was difficult for anyone who had not been through it himself to understand, even when he tried; but when in addition to that a screen of indifference was habitually raised, how completely were the unfortunate ones cut off.

Alphonse now realized that health is the truest form of worldly riches. He saw that between the well and the sick there tends to arise some sort of barrier like that between the rich and the poor. The sick one may soon despair of being able to make the well one realize how he feels, and the well one, on his part, does not wish to probe too much for fear of oppressing with pity. Thus falls the shutout suffering in solitude. It seemed to Alphonse to be in communication that failure took place.

And he recalled a speech he had heard in the Chamber boasting of the railways and telegraph lines.

"We have crossed the Frazer and Mackenzie rivers. We have scaled the Rocky Mountains. We telegraph across the continent."

Speed. Fast travel. You could now send a telegram to someone in San Francisco.

But what if the fellow next door was perishing from loneliness? He could be and often was, though seeing dozens a day, from sheer inability to find even one understanding companion. Communication, indeed! The kind we're getting is on the outside. Real communication should be on the inside.

You had to reach inside a person.

You had to bring persons together.

The thing we call Progress often drives them apart.

Though he ate scarcely at all he experienced a constant feeling of fullness. This mocked him in his weakness. His enforced idleness left him prey to thought, and his pains brought indignation that accumulated to a sense of outrage. And two voices that came from he knew not where warred within him, one with the other. The one was full of rage, bitter, indignant and blasphemous; the other was faint, distant, but serene and equable.

"A man comes into this world without the asking. Then he must suffer pain, poverty, and sickness. Why does God permit this?"

"Man is to grow into a higher being—a spirit. And suffering is a part of the process in the making of a spirit."

"That is a nice old nursery tale. But one cannot grasp it when the hour of suffering falls."

"There is a virtue called patience. Divine. All things come to him . . ."

"What good is it to me now to say, 'if you bear your troubles, you will be a good spirit a hundred years from now'?"

"The present passes quickly. It is your direction that counts."

"Nothing will drive a man in the wrong direction so completely as disaster and pain."

"False anger. It is not disaster and pain which of themselves drive a man to despair. It is how he accepts them. If he knows how to evaluate suffering he recognizes an opportunity."

"If suffering is valuable why didn't God give men immediate perception of that value—as in the case of good food?"

"Then there would be no exercising of faith—and it is only by faith that man can move from being to higher being."

"God the Creator is the one responsible for your existence. You suffer. It is as if he had created you to torment you."

"Not so; He created you to be happy. By enduring through faith the soul is cleansed, gains merit, and is made worthy for eternal life."

"Can you imagine an earthly father seeing his child hungry, sick, alone, stricken with fear and desolation, and not coming to help him? No, you can't! Yet that is what God does."

"It is God who sends, by his implanted love, the human father to the stricken ones."

"You can pray your fingers thin and cry your eyes out in pain. Nothing happens."

"Who knows that nothing happens? A real prayer has faith. Faith makes patience easy. But words and tears may be only an outburst of the self."

"Defy God and curse him and vent your rages and take the pleasure of this expression. It's little enough for what you are going through!" the irreverent voice replied, pouring the bile of bitterness and doubt and despair into his soul. And the quiet, small voice replied back: "That is folly. This bitterness increases with expression. Rather patience."

Thus the endless dialogue of his weak and desolate hours.

The irreverent voice, the strong visualizer of man's woes, often swept all before it with furious impact.

On one such occasion, Alphonse cried out: "God help me!"

Wearied and shaking he tried to rid his mind of the fruitless debate. He prayed that God might send some sign of compassion, some inkling that He even saw. Out of his depths he cried it. Nothing happened. Only the sound of his own voice startled him—its sincerity, its pleadingness, its frankness, bringing home to him his loneliness and absurdity. The abyss had sealed around him.

At such a time the reflection that others, too, suffer, that the world in fact is full of affliction, did not help him. It only added to the sense of bafflement and sorrow. The hospitals, the homes for the aged, the insane asylums, he knew, were full of stricken beings. They differ only in a little degree from anyone else. In their very bones is burning an unwritten history of man. It is as if the hell of the damned in time were intruding upon earth. Must one be damned in time to be saved in eternity? What a strange seesawing was this pattern called salvation! Or was it that the human race bought its way to continuation but by a constant torrent of atonements?

The doctors take careful readings, the method of which is

preserved in their books. They gather clever observations and make laconic marks on a chart and gather statistics: pulse, 80; temperature, 100; blood pressure, so and so. But the anguish of the human heart is without a history. Neither God nor man has ever invented a symbol by which it can be marked down.

Wearied and shaking, he tried to rid his mind of the fruitless doubts.

He desired sleep—as much to find oblivion from mental anguish as rest from bodily weariness.

But when he had dozed a few minutes a fly that had been in a corner of the room flew down to his bed and busied himself with tickling Alphonse's nose, crawling with germ-laden feelers across his lips and buzzing in his ears until he was awakened again to his anguish.

Outside his confessional (which was his forte) was hung the little sign: Abbé Clement. To his friends he was always a haven of refuge, a Franciscan, a man whose humility and profundity encased him in the anonymity of the mystical life, working always through others. He came now to see his friend, Alphonse Desjardins, whom he had heard was sick. What was more natural than that Alphonse should unburden himself in confession; for in this circle of people the state of a man's soul and his relationship with God were regarded as the closest reality.

When there was said what was to be said, Abbé Clement spoke in tones of understanding and compassion: "Sorrow is a passion to avoid. Self-pity can, too, be as blind as anger or hate. While the soul is swept with these passions the grace of God cannot operate.

"These ideas, they come. One cannot help that. But sidestep them as you would a storm. Do not try to meet them head on by reasoning and argument with yourself. Like the storm, they will pass.

"Submit to God's will and pray. Your peace of mind will return quickest in that way.

"Suffering is the most important work to do on earth. It is more important than all that goes on in business, industry, learning, and politics. To take part in an atonement is an essential of being a Christian.

"You were minded to do a good work. God will now bring you to fulfill it through contradiction. Such method is the artistry of the Divine."

When Abbé Clement had departed, Alphonse's attention turned to the doctor who was attending him regularly. He examined Alphonse again and kept asking further questions as to his symptoms. In the meantime he kept up a running commentary upon the progress to health of various of his patients who were known also to the Desjardins. This woman had been delivered of a baby. That boy had bravely outborne a fierce attack of the measles. A man whose back had been broken by a fall down the bucket shaft of a gold mine would never walk again. That was difficult. He had only just married a beautiful girl.

"Cannot you now tell me, doctor, what it is I am suffering from?" Alphonse asked.

The doctor hemmed. The odor of carbolic acid flowed from his person as he folded his stethoscope.

"I have consulted a specialist in Montreal on your case," he said. "Before I have his advice on the reports, it will be a day yet or perhaps two. You lose nothing by this rest in bed."

Alphonse smiled wryly. If a doctor only had some way of weighing what goes through a patient's mind as carefully as he does his urine.

It was spring now. Its breath came through his open window. The south wind was warming the Northland and carrying off the vapors that rose above the river and using them to spray the open mouths of buds upon the awakening earth. The children played upon the dried streets and came home tanned with wind and sun.

There was a languor in the air. Men found it harder to think, and forced themselves to go to work. The robins returned in

flocks and sang on the lawns at dawn. All day the call of an
unknown bird could be heard even through the noise of the city,
though the bird remained incommunicado in its chosen grove.

Light and sunshine drenched the earth. On all sides life was
calling. Alphonse thought of the dark cold of December and
that then it had been easier to stay indoors crouched beneath
his blankets. But now all renewals were to the outside—to out-
going and the open road. How ruthless was the hand that smote!

Across the street the husky grocer fretted behind his counter.
He noticed a slower turnover in his goods. People would run
up bills all winter and forget about you in the spring, he thought.
Give them credit when they come to you with their tongues out
and you'll soon have to close your doors. He ragged his clerks
and quarreled with his brother over a division of the profits.

In the same block, Lyette the milkman fumed at the lateness
of the hour and the time it was taking for him to get through
his route. There was too much talk at some of the back doors
where talkative housewives detained him with bits of gossip. It
was hard on the horses but he cursed them just the same and laid
on the whip.

He had no time to express sympathetic sentiments about
Monsieur Alphonse Desjardins being sick. A man had been
stricken in his tracks, that's all. Not by an animal. Not by his
fellow man. But by Nature, or God. That was it. No use to
cudgel the brain over such happenings.

The warm, humid winds of spring buffeted his passage to the
doorways. His back had been itchy ever since he'd taken off his
long underwear, and this warm spring air was giving him prickly
heat. The breakage on his bottles was going up. The more
business you had the tougher it got. A man couldn't make much
of a living in the milk business, that was plain, Lyett said to
himself. A necessary food some called it, yes, and there were
some that didn't have it at all, but they'd all slam the door in a
fellow's face quick enough. Bah!

Well, life was a dirty game, that's sure. To hell with it! Come Saturday night he would go on a damned good spree at the Sign of the Swinging Door, the hottest tavern in old Quebec.

As for Alphonse he, at that very moment, had become invested with an awareness in utter defiance of all account books and double-entry bookkeeping methods.

The bitter mood had passed. He had a clean-swept feeling. An indescribable peace had entered into him. There had come to him an experience of ineffable sweetness within, beyond all logic, beyond all will and effort, beyond all cataloguing and explanation, but more real than the scrawny and labored nibbles at reality that come to the human mind through arithmetic, philosophy, and science. This infusion by-passed years of the labors of the mind, all accumulations of learning and memory.

It was a mode of knowing that becalmed all other ways of perception. It was simply a Presence.

His soul was free. He sang. He found moving within him a buoyant energy of the intellect.

Thus did Alphonse feel that the Lord God of Hosts follows no human method of bookkeeping and that those who are supposed to be unhappy are not necessarily unhappy.

Chapter 8

"Why, Dorimène, I did not realize it! I wouldn't know Alphonse. He scared me. I couldn't believe my eyes."

It was Napoleon, the younger brother. He had a job that took him to Ottawa, and he had not seen Alphonse for quite a while. He was excited.

"It just goes on and on," said Dorimène, trying to rub the sleep from her eyes. "One day at a time. I am always afraid of what the next will bring."

Napoleon had thought that Dorimène was one of the most beautiful women in the world when Alphonse had married her. Now her face was lined and her hair graying. He pitied her.

"And such a blow for you, Dorimène. With the children. All this worry. My God!"

"The children, they are healthy," said Dorimène, who could see one bright gleam.

"He is so thin," said Napoleon, who couldn't take his mind off the way Alphonse looked. "Well, when I came to the door I saw him. He drooped. And he used to be so straight!"

"It is very sad."

"Dorimène, tell me, is there not something I can do? What is his doctor saying now?"

And Dorimène replied: "He says he is at his wits' end with him. He is very sorry but there is nothing more he can do. He thinks it is his liver. There is only one man he can think of that might do something for him. He is a specialist in Montreal."

Alphonse would have to go there. Nothing further could be done for him in Lévis. But how could it be managed? Someone would have to accompany him.

With her flair for decisiveness in a crisis, Dorimène solved this. She placed their children out among friends. She closed the house.

"My place is at your side," she told him when he fretted about the children. "What do you think I married you for? Was it not for better or for worse?"

She put Alphonse on the train and went with him to Montreal.

Alphonse felt stimulated. He was glad his malady was not one that was going to confine him to straight bed rest. The bustle and hurry of the railway coach aroused in him a sense of being normal after his days in bed.

He felt hopeful now, though his legs were wobbly and the swift motion of the train made him a little dizzy until he became used to it.

The coach was not filled, and they were able to occupy a section and talk without other listeners. The excitement of travel revived Alphonse's strength and good spirits. But he could not get the children out of his mind.

"It will be strange for them in other beds," he said ruefully. "They will be crying at night."

"Don't worry about it," Dorimène said. "At their age they cry over any little thing. But really they are too young to stay sad about anything very long."

"Just the same a sad and baffled look on one of those little faces hurts more than any pain I know. It is perhaps the thought that they are just beginners in the suffering of the world they will yet have to face."

Outside was the rich farmland. The train sped over the level plain that had been wet-nursed a thousand years in its roots by the overspill of the river. Before their eyes passed farm after farm, with white houses and great barns and the rich green of new life breaking in the fields, cattle standing in the grass, and flocks of sheep with young lambs romping and playful in the sun.

"It is not well for you to be having such thoughts at this time," Dorimène chided.

"Ah, Dorimène, it is not that I am sad when I say that. Though I will admit that when we pity a child's sorrow we are pitying ourselves a little, too. They are beginning the journey that we have half finished. But what I want to say is this: There is a happiness that comes above this sadness. It takes it in, like a spicing in the cake, and comes all above it in the end.

"There are many who do not want the spicing, as you call it. They want the joy of life and nothing else."

"Yes, that's the way it is," said Alphonse. "But we must believe they lose a good chance for themselves that way—the chance to grow."

When the train stopped at a little country station, Alphonse and Dorimène could see out into a strip of pastureland where sheep were grazing. The ewes cast anxious glances at the locomotive and bleated toward a little band of lambs which gamboled and pranced and flicked their tails in the careless ecstasy of their newborn legs.

Alphonse and Dorimène gazed at the lambs, admiring the joyous meekness of their faces and their happiness at the gift of life. And they, for a moment, were without words.

Dorimène was next to speak, slowly, for she too had now caught his mood. The renewings of life and the beauties of the spring day that lay open around them had touched her, awakening an imponderable nostalgia and arousing suddenly in her mind age-old speculation on the wonder and meaning of existence.

"Have you ever thought, Alphonse," she said, "why it is that the young are so beautiful? I remember when I was a child there was a little pup at the house of a friend where I used to go often. He was cute and eager and full of winning ways. Then for years I did not see him. And when I did he was old and so sort of ugly, my goodness, I did not know him and I said to my friend: 'where is Jumbo now?' And my friend said: 'That's Jumbo. Here, Jumbo, come, come on now and see the lady. Nice doggie!'

"Oh, my goodness! And when I saw those lambs back there it all came into my mind again. And it is the same with human beings. Look at those in the homes for the aged. Think of the poor wizened old folks and how at one time they were such sweet babies and the pride of their mothers and fathers. *Why are the young so beautiful?*"

Dorimène was on the verge of tears and Alphonse had now to comfort her.

"Ah, now, Dorimène, you were chiding me for 'such thoughts,' as you called them. Now you put a very heavy one indeed to me. But is it not that the beauty of the young is a physical beauty and is bestowed by the Creator independent of ourselves? Life in this world takes it from us.

"But there is another beauty, too, called moral beauty. This we are able to make ourselves. It is this only that we can have when life's end comes. No one can take it from us."

"It is true, I am sure," said Dorimène. "When you look at it in that light the sadness goes out of it. For no one is meant to stay long on this earth; that is clear. But it is hard to grasp; it is hard to see the moral beauty."

"It must be for us to find it out," said Alphonse. "The more we think frankly and unafraid along these lines the more we see that religion is part of life. Moral beauty is many things, but most of all living to help one's kind."

"The need of religion is a fact. Why, it is the most real thing we know—if one follows through at all to the great questions . . ." Dorimène's voice trailed off.

"Religion is the true realism—if, as you say, there is the follow-through. Well spoken."

"The skeptics, though, think of it as something unreal."

"Yes, and there are those in some journalistic and literary

circles who call themselves realists," said Alphonse. "And what is their realism? Well, they dote on the memoirs of courtesans; they peep over transoms; they report adulteries. They would like to appear blasé but really they are green-struck bards of the navel. One would think that there was not more to life than that."

"It is profitable to write that, I suppose," said Dorimène. "And writers feel they have to make money as well as other men."

They fell silent then.

But Alphonse was thinking deeply. After a little while he said: "Do you remember the first evening when we walked up the cliff at Lévis?"

"I will never forget it."

"And when we were looking at the shabby houses and the hungry children I told you that I wanted to be able to do something in my lifetime to help such people."

"Yes, Alphonse, you did not want others to pass through what you had to pass through."

"Well, I am a failure," he said evenly. "So far, I have done nothing."

"Not a failure. How can you say it? You've the family—and the house."

"The family and the house! They are good. I thank God for them. But is the lot of the workers aided by one having a comfortable home and family? That is the question. If I recover? *If I recover?*"

"Of course you will recover," she said earnestly. "You will have your health back. You will have another job. And then when the children are older you will be able to pay more attention to your dream."

And she talked to cheer him with hopeful thoughts for the future, for she knew that this dream was close to his heart and she feared his too-close preoccupation with it when his real struggle was still for health.

The four-hour journey passed quickly. Soon the gray stone shapes of Montreal began to appear.

They went at once to the home of a friend to whom Dorimène had written. There was a quiet room where Alphonse could rest and await the hour of his appointment with the famous doctor.

The man who sat next to Alphonse spoke first. He asked Alphonse if the doctor were really in, so slow was the movement among the line-up of waiting patients. Alphonse said he thought he was and went on looking at the large framed picture opposite on the wall which revealed that Doctor Amos P. Henry (along with many others) had in 1885 graduated with merit from Harvard Medical School.

But something in the man's voice had aroused his curiosity. There seemed to be smacking noises in the back of his mouth when he spoke. He looked now and saw a man of about fifty-five, of thin face and work-worn frame; his eyes, though heavy, had still more than a trace of that youthful freshness that survives longest in those manual workers who live close to the land and nature. He was a little excited and obviously wanted to compare notes with another fellow patient.

"He's a great man," he said. "There's no doubt about it—and it's when you have to wait so long you know it."

Alphonse did not see any necessary connection between greatness and keeping someone in want waiting. The waiting, he hoped, was an accident. It was just the sort of point that he, when younger, would have argued with his teacher and gotten in a little wrong.

Aloud he said: "They say he is a good doctor. I don't know, but I hope so."

"Of course, me, you know," said the man with a new outbreak of smacking in his voice, "I've been to three others. All of them could do nothing for me." In this his pride almost equaled his disappointment. "It was them that sent me here."

"Then you've been sick for some time?" Alphonse asked.

"Nigh on two years," he said. My name's Henry Treeser. I've a farm near Huntingdon, P.Q. Y' know in the first six months it took near all our savings, what with doctor's bills and medicine and me not workin'."

Alphonse liked this lean, talkative man. And it relieved the tension of waiting for a doctor to hear another man tell his troubles. He let sympathy be in his face when the words did not come easily. He looked now along the row of chairs at the other patients, wondering what tale of woe everyone concealed under his courage.

"And your family?" he enquired. "Are they all right?"

"There's but the wife now," the man replied. "Our boy's married and gone out West. He's gettin' a family of his own now."

"It's good that there are no small ones."

"It's good that way, yes. If I can only hold on to the home is what bothers me."

"You mean that? . . ."

"Y' see, it's like this. We've been borrowin'. After about six months our cash was gone and I heard of a loan company. I thought it plumb convenient at the time—humph!" His voice died down in a series of small smackings and clatters inside his mouth and he seemed to swallow with a little difficulty as if his tonsils were too thick.

Then he continued in a lowered voice: "Three loans I got in all. Of course, I didn't make no payments, and that compound interest, how it did gather! When I got the bill here a month back I owed near as much again as I had borrowed. And it's still goin' on."

For all of that, Mr. Treeser was genial and there was no trace of bitterness in him, which aroused Alphonse's interest the more. As he listened to the man talk, Alphonse thought that he was like one born to the vocation of getting the dirty end of things; when the doctor's receptionist called his own name he was a little reluctant to part with this humble man who took the blows as if they were his inheritance.

Even when Doctor Henry was examining him and asking questions, there was one thought cutting in on his mind when, he reflected, he should be thinking of other things.

"Compound interest, how it did gather!"

How it did gather. That sounded like some malady, too. Some malignant growth eating into a man's vitals.

Doctor Henry's examination was thorough, his advice discreet.

"In cases of the liver," he said, "such as yours, our main treatment is diet. Often the results are excellent. I will have to have you in the hospital for some further observations and to get you started on it."

Alphonse was cheered and relieved. He began to have hopes that the money they had saved up would see them through till he could go back to work.

"And after some days . . . I will be able to go home?" Alphonse asked.

"We cannot always say for sure but we will hope so." The doctor's voice was honest and strong and he spoke with gusto.

He used his own strength, Alphonse thought, to spark others with hope to fight for theirs. They hit it off right from the start.

The treatment which Alphonse received in Montreal soon started him on the road back to health. After a few days of comfortable progress in the hospital and the establishment of his new diet, he had made such improvement that Dorimène returned to Lévis. She had begun to get lonesome for the children, and Alphonse insisted that she should go. He hoped to follow in a matter of weeks.

Gradually his symptoms cleared up. Light exercise was prescribed. He began to gain in weight and get his color back. Frequently he walked in the corridors and became acquainted with other patients.

One day, in passing a ward far removed, he spied Henry Treeser, his friend of the waiting room.

The lean man was genial as ever. "You look better already," he said. "I kin see a big change."

"I guess I'm lucky after all," said Alphonse.

"And you? Are you on the mend?"

"I've a chance," he said. "The doctor says I've a fighting chance. But with the hospital treatment and all—I've had to make over the farm."

"You had to do that! To whom."

"To the loan company. I signed the deed this morning." And there was a little clatter at the butt of his tongue.

"You didn't think," said Alphonse, "of going to some trusted friend for—for the loan?"

" 'T wasn't that I didn't think of it. But a feller hates to embarrass a friend like that, and this loan company they keeps everything secret that way."

"Oh, yes, it's a secret." The quality of Alphonse's tones was lost upon Treeser, who could only think of the loss of his land and home.

"Y' know," he went on, "a feller gets 'tached to his land when he's worked it for nigh on to forty years." The man who had been carefree had a sob in his voice now and there were tears in his eyes. He was beginning to whine and his spirit was breaking.

Alphonse did not know what to say. He tried to tell Henry Treeser that when he got his health back he would soon earn enough to pay off his debts. Halfway through he remembered the compound interest and how it did gather, and he knew that he was wrong. This man Treeser was licked. His medical costs were going on at rates of interest he would never be able to pay. Financially the man was in quicksand. The thought saddened and angered Alphonse, and he went darkly to his bed.

What kind of world was it when one enemy struck a man down, and as he was fighting, another kind of enemy came and moved in fast to finish him while he was weak?

Chapter 9

ALPHONSE woke up in the early morning light. God, it was good to be back in his own room in his own house above the cliff.

This long convalescence made you a poor sleeper. It was a time to think in the early morning, before Dorimène had stirred and before the children came to with their clatter. In months of it you had plenty of time, and found yourself winding through the same questions.

If men suffered illness, if they came into affliction and poverty, why did it happen that somehow a veil of secrecy was drawn around them?

From the pulpits in the churches it was said that the Cross was noble. It was the way of Christ, Himself. Some called it the Royal Road.

But outside the Church men ran from it. Those who had poverty tended to hide it. Those who didn't have it feared it. They all ran from suffering in the raw. Submission to the Cross was the great exhortation—as long as it was the other fellow who was under it. It was as if all saw in suffering some humiliating defeat of all humanity. Yet suffering was the commonest thing on earth—the one common cord that ran into all ages and stations of life.

He had heard it said of the early Christians shortly after the time of Christ that some of them prayed they might be afflicted, so much was suffering esteemed among them. He felt that in such a circle and with such an attitude, suffering would be much more easily borne than in the modern world—which sees glory in suffering only in the case of such heroes as the soldiers and sailors who receive their wounds in fighting wars.

The modern world found in the very thought of suffering a stumbling block. Suffering snagged progress. Suffering let an awful-looking cat out of the bag. The denial of suffering made it all the harder to bear.

Yes, the mask must come off. Those who suffered poverty or pain should make their condition known. But supposing they did—and they found only that they had embarrassed a friend, as Henry Treeser had feared. This could only add to their unhappiness.

So there you were with no answer. Only worse than before.

Was mankind to quail forever and forever be baffled before this black pit of suffering on the earth?

Quash it! He'd get out today and walk as the doctor ordered; he'd go to Quebec on the ferryboat and look around. Maybe he'd bump into some former friends of the Green Chamber.

Later, when he had pleasantly fatigued himself on the steep streets of the old city, he turned into the library. Now was the time to read, he thought, as he came to the long tables.

"On my word, I'm most glad to see you back, Alphonse Despardins." It was bearded old Felix Desbarres, who had just peered out from behind a stack of books on the table.

"Sit down, man, sit down. It is not every day that I have a chance to greet in person a man who has left a standard in the recording of public documents which our province should not forget in a generation."

Alphonse smiled and pulled up a chair. It was good to meet a man of conversation. Old Felix, the book critic, he had known in newspaper days.

"Leave it to a literary critic like yourself," he said, "to recognize something or other in a document."

Old Felix closed his notebook. He lowered his voice before he spoke again, as if more to himself.

"It is, perhaps, something that a man does not wish to remember—a dismissal like that. Oh, politics!"

"I have been sick, my dear Felix. A long sickness. A battle of.
another kind into which I have been putting my forces. I do not
want to recall events that might send more bile swooshing into
the belly."

"Ha, ha!" said old Felix. "Rather I would say you have the
instinct to defend the serenity of your own mind. That is
splendid. More splendid than you know. For the day will come
when you will serve only what you think is right, not what
people think or say about you."

"Now you flatter me. Go away."

"Do you know one of the main curses of our public and
political life is that men have their hearts eaten out alive by
rivalries of factions!" Felix asserted. "After awhile they can't
think straight."

"Well, anyhow," said Alphonse, "I've had another experience.
I've been plunged into different things. It reminded me of my
father's ill-health, and what can happen to a family when the
breadwinner is struck. That, I tell you, is something in our
country. There was a man in the hospital with me. He lost
everything he owned."

"No money?"

"No credit. Went to a moneylender. And lost his farm."

While Felix stroked his beard, Alphonse told him what had
happened to Harry Treeser when the farmer's health got bad.

"That reminds me," said Felix, reaching out on the library table
to pick up his brief case. "You mention moneylending. Have
you ever heard of a man by the name of—what is it now? I
have just read about his work in a paper from Paris last week.
Yes, here is the piece. A German named Friedrich Wilhelm
Raiffeisen. He saw the effects of this moneylending in his own
country."

"What did he do?"

"He formed societies of credit for those who needed it. Let me see now. Shall I read a little to you?"

"That is interesting. Tell me about it."

"Usury was condemned by Moses in the Old Law because it gave the rich too much of a stranglehold on the poor," observed Felix, adjusting his glasses.

"Well the gist of it is this: About thirty years ago, moneylenders, cattle buyers, and land brokers were exploiting the rural people in Germany. This man, Raiffeisen, set up about one hundred credit societies in the Rhine Province. They were to loan money to the needy at the lowest possible rate of interest. He wanted to give the people something which would help them to fight these evils. He was nearly blind when he entered into this work."

"Blind?"

"Raiffeisen was a burgomaster. He went to visit a sick person and caught typhoid fever. It left his sight bad. He had to give up his office as burgomaster. Then, going blind, he started these societies and gave all his time and energy to them. They were for the poor."

"How strange! How very strange!" Alphonse hauled in his feet and sat straight up in his chair. He had lost his feeling of fatigue. "Does it say anything else about him?" he asked.

"Oh, yes. He was a plain, simple man. One of a family of nine. He was of the Protestant faith. But Catholic priests came to see him and get his advice. It was his works of charity that drew all. But here, you take the copy with you and read it all if you wish. You can mail it back to me in a few days."

There was a noise at the head desk. The librarian had his topcoat on. It was closing time.

"I would be glad to," said Alphonse. Outside they parted.

The ferryboat rose and fell gently, a cradle rocked by the arm of Ocean in the St. Lawrence. Alphonse picked a quiet seat and his eyes sought the rest of the article that Felix Desbarres had given him. The author had quoted from Raiffeisen himself:

The society aims less at obtaining business profits than the strengthening of the economically weak and the furtherance of the intellectual and moral well-being of its members.

The only means to eliminate selfishness is the practice of Christianity in public life. Now is the time to express this thought openly and to strive earnestly for its realization.

If I, as spokesman, emphasize this consideration at a meeting of a purely economic character, I thereby leave aside all denominational distinctions and stress only the principles common to Christian denominations. Primarily, however, I have in mind that Christian charity which, based on love of God, constitutes the basis of the constitution, in fact of the entire organization of the loan association. Without it the society will be incapable of salutary activity.

"Whatever ye have done unto the least of these my brethren, ye have done unto Me." These words of our Saviour constitute the basis of the loan associations and their organization.

Raiffeisen, the writer concluded, knew enough about the world to see that nothing was more against virtue than hapless poverty and misery. He turned to the co-operative idea because it could stifle selfishness and sought moral improvements in economic conduct.

Slowly Alphonse walked up the cliff. Slowly past the places where despair had stripped shame from humanity, past where he had confided to Dorimène years before that he would do something yet to help his people. Quash it! What a failure was Alphonse Desjardins!

It was late. He knew it.

"I've had your diet fixed an hour ago. You know what too much exercise might do." Dorimène's voice held a reproving note.

"I was resting and reading in the library. Not strenuous that."

But he went early to bed, past all reproaches and the children's noises.

That half-blind burgomaster over in Germany! He had seen the moneylenders and the traders sucking blood. If a man is being robbed in one part of the world he may put out his hand and pick up a weapon. If a man is being robbed in another part of the world he may put out his hand and pick up the same weapon.

Oh, God, I remember, too, there were things I wanted to do. Things that I told Dorimène. Things that I have yet to do.

Had the half-blind burgomaster ever known anyone like Henry Treeser? Of course he had. The world was full of Henry Treesers.

Could one man speak to another across the world? Without words?

Now, in the case of Henry, there had been this: Henry had not wanted to embarrass, as he had said, his friends by asking for a loan and so had fallen into the clutches of the usurers. Mulling it over in his mind, Alphonse reflected that his friends would be just as embarrassed going to Henry and offering him help.

There was a touchiness about these things: it was what put the noose on the isolated little man. Then, as he pondered, Alphonse, too, saw the answer. Why, of course, there ought to be a regular little organization within the community that would be the go-between.

Then he saw clearly another reason. In every community— or rather, parish, which was the unit in which he thought—there are lots of good, kind people who want to chip in with their neighbors when any kind of trouble comes. But each one's will to help is separated from the other's, and one doesn't even realize that the other feels that way. And the little individual anyway is not able to do much alone. But what if the so-disposed came together and were banded in a regular little institution run by themselves? Then there would be a regular field-going organism to succor the needy.

Why, in every parish of Quebec there ought to be one such. The more Alphonse studied the question, the more convinced he became.

From his writings it was certain, too, that Raiffeisen was not thinking of any impersonal service. The area that each society should serve should be restricted, he said. The members must know each other. They should know the economic condition of each family well enough and whether or not a man was a good worker. They would know each other's character without tramping on a fellow's toes. With this knowledge, and above all with the idea of the second great commandment of Christ that must be taught, should it not be possible to have a pool of credit?

These thoughts Alphonse kept in his mind. For many days he kept them. His health improved. His neighbors on Guenette Street in Lévis were saying that he was looking like his old self again and it was so good to see him getting better. What fine medicine was it that brought this recovery, or was it, perhaps, due to the intercession of *la bonne Sainte Anne?*

To which Alphonse would reply, it was the diet. As far as he could see it was the diet which the Montreal doctor had changed and which Dorimène was so anxious to see that he carried out. And what was that diet, was it permissible to enquire?

"It is very simple," Alphonse would reply. It is, "Eat the carrot."

They would all laugh a little, not knowing that it was a joke.

Then Alphonse would say: "Believe me, when I am all better I do not wish even to pass by a field of carrots for some time."

At this they would laugh a little more. Usually someone would ask: "It is this that the great specialist of Montreal has advised?"

"Eat the carrot. Yes!"

"How marvelous!"

It made everyone feel good that a fellow could get his health back in such a simple way, and the wiser ones, though they suspected there was more to it than that, didn't let on.

When he was able to work again it was natural that his mind turned to the job he had lost. He had recorded and published for eleven years the debates in the Quebec legislature. Then, because he wouldn't change the record for an important politician who had put his feet into his mouth, he had been dismissed. He tried to keep it out of his mind but it kept coming back.

Was it that he had been too honorable? Dorimène had said that more than once, though not by way of censure.

He kept putting the thought of it out of his mind. He didn't want to think of those happenings. All he wanted was his health. Every night he and Dorimène and the children held family prayers. He wanted to get his mind free of anything that would make him bitter. He had an instinct for defending the serenity of his own mind, Felix Desbarres had said. He would guard that. It was a good instinct that.

Soon his new chance came. His record in the Green Chamber did not go unnoticed. In the very next year the post of French-language stenographic clerk in the House of Commons at Ottawa became vacant.

Who could be found to fill it? The number of men able to do this exacting work was not great. The name of Alphonse Desjardins was soon proposed. He was qualified by experience. Of the probity of his record-making there had been a demonstration, *sans doute*.

Dorimène gave her consent in the end. He would have to be in Ottawa during all sessions of the Parliament, and this she did not like. He would make $2,000 a year and there would be some leisure time, which she felt would be good in view of his health.

"But we will keep the home in Lévis," she said. "The home that we have built together."

"It's the only thing to do," said Alphonse. "But I won't be living at all when I'm away from here. It'll be just work and a room to stay in."

"But you will write often?" coaxed Dorimène. "When you are absent, what will it be here? Just keeping a house."

"I will write when I am absent," he said. "I will write you every day, I tell you, while I am in Ottawa."

Chapter 10

NAPOLEON DESJARDINS rolled up the newspaper tightly and walked out on the street. He was headed for Alphonse's apartment.

Alphonse must not miss that one. It was the *Revue des deux Mondes* published in Paris, and it had an article on co-operation. He knew that Alphonse was studying during all the time he could spare in Ottawa and his summers at home in Lévis.

Napoleon remembered his brother insisting on getting this quiet place to live when he had first come; then how he shifted his desk to the place where it would receive the most light and placed his few books on it. With a house and family to keep in Lévis, he couldn't afford more anyhow. Well, thought Napoleon, even on a holiday like today when I would like to go to the·ball game, Alphonse will have his nose into those books, if he has not already gone to the library.

But Alphonse himself answered his knock.

"Ah, Napoleon, it's you. Come in. Glad to see you."

"I've brought the *Revue des deux Mondes*, which has an article on co-operation," said Napoleon. He looked at his brother, marveling at how he had recovered his health, though his face was thinner these last years.

"Good. But before I read it let me tell you something. There has been a discussion in the House of Commons on usury. A lot of talk and some startling figures."

"I have some figures on that myself," said Napoleon. " I know a fellow, a civil servant here in Ottawa. He borrowed twenty dollars. He paid one dollar a month on it in interest. What's that now? Sixty per cent on a yearly basis. He paid the dollar every month for thirty months: thirty dollars.

"Sounds fantastic! It really happened?" asked Alphonse.

"Absolutely. I tell you the truth. Not only that. He was sued for the original twenty dollars. There was no end to it."

"That's as bad an instance as any I've heard in the House," said Alphonse. "Several members have stated that fifty or sixty per cent is not unusual. Of course, when a man gets caught in this sort of thing he is usually in a jam of some kind and doesn't like to tell about it."

"That's what they take advantage of."

"It's like one of the members said. The loan shark was a real menace. But what could be done about him? If the little citizen ran to the shark for a loan and agreed to pay the rate, and in the hurry of his need signed any piece of paper that was poked under his nose, it was mighty hard to keep a check on all that."

"Well, what about the banks?" asked Napoleon. He stretched out his feet and leaned back in his chair. Might as well forget about the ball game now. "Did anyone ask about the banks in the debate?"

"Yes, during the discussion, which was rather long, the banks came in. They argued about the whole thing pro and con. And I took it down for *Hansard*."

Napoleon's eyes grew large. What a position of trust his brother held! Why, *Hansard* was a national institution. One slip there, mister, and what a commotion! You wouldn't be safe.

How proud he had been of Alphonse when first he saw him at that listening post in the Commons! No one knew more about the politicians. You had to be a genius for sure to catch that flow of words and sometimes, Napoleon felt, of folly. But Alphonse, he was always respectful. These were the tribunes of the people, he would say modestly.

"Go on. Tell me about it," said Napoleon.

"I will, if the thumb can stand it," replied Alphonse, laughing. It was a standing joke between the brothers, how Napoleon cut his thumb years before helping Alphonse build his house.

"I shed my blood for that house," Napoleon laughed back. "It can stand anything now. Go ahead."

He gave a glance at the thumb just the same and tried the joint.

"Well, naturally, during the discussion," began Alphonse, "someone asked, what about the banks? Wasn't that part of their business, the loaning of money?"

"Yes, there were the banks. The banks were commercial; their doors were open to the public all alike. They had their patrons' deposits to think about. Yes, they gave loans on good security; they ran on a regular set of rules and couldn't be expected to jeopardize their patrons' deposits by loaning money willy-nilly to anyone that came in with a hard luck story and needed a loan real bad.

"Banks, being only in the business of banking, would soon go broke if they did that. It was obvious and everybody agreed. Nothing was worse in a country than to have the banks failing and losing the people's savings. Everybody agreed to that, too.

"The banks served business. If you had liquid assets, you could always get a loan from the bank—if you knew the manager and had acceptable security. The banks had enough to do, doing what they were doing according to banking principles. And the first of these principles is that banking is not philanthropy."

Liquid assets? What were they? Napoleon wanted to know.

They were, Alphonse said, something that could be readily turned into cash. In other words a fellow who didn't need a loan very badly could get a loan. That was it. That was the trouble. "To him that hath shall be given . . ."

But the great majority of people didn't have bank accounts; didn't know a bank manager from Adam. But they knew their neighbors in the villages and their neighbors knew them. Too, lots of them lived thirty miles away from where a commercial bank found it profitable to operate.

There was a place for something else. For another kind of bank, if you will. There should be no need, he said, of running foul of the existing banks.

Napoleon listened to his brother with growing admiration. His sessions there in the Commons had given him an insight, sure enough. He knew the how and the why of things now. And in his studies he never stopped, and what was more, he never rushed. That made Napoleon feel in awe of him; though he feared his brother's idealism could lead him into trouble, he did not feel that he was equal to arguing with him on such a deep problem of the people.

"I'm hungry, Alphonse," he said at last. "Let us go out and have lunch."

When they came back, Napoleon slept a while. When he awoke Alphonse had just finished reading the article in the *Revue des deux Mondes*.

Alphonse stroked back his long handlebar moustache. "Ah, yes, Napoleon, why has there not been started a similar movement among our people in Quebec? You know, I thought for a time of co-operative bakery in Lévis. Then I thought of co-operative insurance. But it is not only that your ideal be right. You've got to be able to carry through and make a success in practice. You've got to be practical, too."

Then they got into a talk on the Rochdale pioneers in England and their system of patron-owned stores.

"It strikes me as an example of what people can do when they work together," Alphonse said. "It is not to say that their system need be copied in every respect. The need in another country might be different. In Italy and Germany now they are forming thrift and credit societies. In Germany there are two types: the Raiffeisen and the Schulze-Delitzsch. Actually the first credit so-

ciety was formed in 1848 by François Haeck, a Belgian, and its
name was Union du Crédit de Bruxelles. The Boerenbund of Belgium is one of our best models. The Rochdale pioneers opened
their first store in 1844. These beginnings were all by the poor
working-class people, wage earners and farmers, led by a few
men who had the interest of these classes at heart."

"I suppose it has not been started in Quebec because no one
knew about it," said Napoleon.

"Yet we have in the parish an ideal starting place for such a
thing," said Alphonse. "It is because no one has thought about
it, as you say."

"It would get a person into all kinds of trouble, that," said
Napoleon. "The poor do not work together well."

"Must we say, my brother, that what other people are doing
we cannot do?" Alphonse countered. "Would it not depend upon
how much time and effort would be put into the work?"

"Just the same, how much thanks would anyone get?"

"If the work proved its worth to the people, the thanks could
take care of itself. It is not going ahead among the small property
owners and workers of these other countries for nothing."

"Then you think it waits for someone to break the ice." Napoleon looked at his brother closely, for he knew what he was thinking. The face was not the chubby Alphonse of his younger days.
An indefinable spiritual quality stood out in the thinner face.

"Well, it would be a case of breaking the ice and then staying
with it," Alphonse said, and he got up on his feet and began
to pace the floor in his narrow sitting room.

"You know," he went on, "the credit society is what is most
needed in Quebec. Most of our people are honest and industrious.
But they haven't got the tools to work with. And there is no
way where the little man can borrow at an economic rate."

"But what model have you to go by? You say there are different types in Europe. How would you know which one would
suit here?"

"I have been studying that matter," Alphonse admitted. "I will explain to you the two main types I've been thinking of—the Raiffeisen and the Schulze-Delitzsch—and the difference between them. In the Raiffeisen system, deposits were not accepted. They were for the very poor and the bank borrowed money from outside its members and loaned to its members. Careful attention is given to the purpose of the loans, and to the character building of the members. The earnings of the society are not divided but are kept as social capital—which in time can make the society independent of outside capital."

Napoleon, during this description, held his peace. To him banking was an abstruse and mysterious business; when he approached the wicket of a real bank, it was always with a sense of awe at the exact and methodical being inside who presumably never made a mistake. But he was feeling proud of his brother's knowledge. Just the same he wanted to show him all the obstacles that would come up in any such dream as Alphonse's.

"Now, the Schulze-Delitzsch model," Alphonse went on, "is a little different. Those banks sell shares to their members and take deposits from members, too. They even take deposits from nonmembers. They will also loan money to nonmembers. As long as the borrower is able to repay his loan they don't worry much about the purpose of the loan. In some ways they are more like an ordinary bank than the Raiffeisen. But they are both cooperative banks in which anyone may join."

"The first one that you described," said Napoleon, "does it loan money to anyone that comes along, or do all have to be members?"

"They have to be members," Alphonse said. "In these—that is, the Raiffeisen banks—there is a strong moral basis developed in the character of the members. They are neighbors, you know, in small groups and know each other well. That is very fine."

"But," said Napoleon, "when this bank wants to loan money to one of its members who has none on deposit, it has first to go and borrow that money from somewhere else, is it not so?"

"Yes," Alphonse said, "and they have to pay interest on it too."

"Exactly."

"That is their weakness. They are not loaning their own money. In this respect I like the Schulze banks better. They encourage their members to thrift by putting in deposits and having them buy shares. They are good in that way, but on the other hand they lack the emphasis on character and neighborhood solidarity that the Raiffeisen has."

Napoleon would have preferred to change the subject by now but he was moved by his brother's intense interest in the matter. For as they talked, more ideas came to Alphonse and his face lit up.

"Do you not see it, Napoleon?" he cried. "A new type of society could be set up. One that had the good qualities of both and left out the poor qualities."

"Just what would that mean?"

"Combine the thrift and savings features of the Schulze with the membership and character basis of the Raiffeisen. Put the two together."

"And where would you start such a business?"

Alphonse stopped. He lowered his head to think deeply.

"It is to be on the basis of neighborhood and a community bond and knowing each other; it should be started among friends," he said slowly. "Why, yes, of course, among friends."

"That would be right where you lived or among those that you worked with?" asked Napoleon.

"Why, look here," said Alphonse, "the more one talks about this the clearer it becomes. I have this idea: in the Province of Quebec the parish is the main unit of social organization. For the reasons we have just said, the parish is, of all places, the right place to start the people's bank. This thing belongs, I tell you, right there in the parishes of Quebec."

Napoleon would say no more. He was for keeping his fingers crossed.

Nearly every time they got together, whether it was at Alphonse's quarters or in Napoleon's house, the brothers had talks on these things.

Their mother had lived with Napoleon during her last years, and when she had died, at a good old age, all the brothers were at the funeral. Napoleon got them together afterward and had a picture taken.

Napoleon was Alphonse's youngest brother. There was a strong bond between these two. Napoleon, who at one time was assistant Deputy Minister of Public Works, liked to help Alphonse in his social and economic studies.

He wrote to a large number of publishing houses in France for catalogues of all their books. In time he had a big stock on hand.

"These I have gathered for you," he said, handing them to Alphonse one day when the latter had come to his house for dinner.

"Ah, that is most kind of you, Napoleon, and I thank you."

Alphonse loaded his pipe, and soon the smoke was coiling about his big head.

The doorbell rang and Napoleon admitted several of his friends. Among them was M. Blondin, a joker and singer of funny songs, and his daughter Evangeline, a charming young girl.

"You do not need to thank me," Napoleon resumed the conversation with his brother. "I have never forgotten the present you once brought home to me. I was about ten years old and had been very sick. You were working on the newspaper in Quebec, and one evening you brought me home a colored toy horse."

Alphonse chuckled. "A small matter, Napoleon, to remember

over so long a time. But that is the way. Sometimes it is the small matters that stick. How funny children are!"

Alphonse had become pensive. "Not long ago," he went on, "I had to punish one of my little ones for disobedience at home. Now Dorimène writes me that this same little one is quite sick."

Napoleon saw the tears gather in Alphonse's eyes, and he looked toward the kitchen.

"Will you carve the chicken, Alphonse?"

"Sure."

Alphonse went to the table and the men gathered around. Evangeline was persuaded to take a seat near Alphonse.

The men were all hungry. The odor of roast chicken made them eager to eat.

But when Alphonse reached to serve Evangeline first she stopped him. "No, no, *merci*. I could not take a thing!"

Alphonse looked surprised. "Oh, but you must," he said.

"No. I have already eaten."

"Not even one small bite? After all you are the only lady of the party."

"Thank you. I couldn't."

Alphonse laid his knife and fork down upon the plate, and looked around at the hungry men.

"If this lady does not eat," he said, "then, *no one eats*." It was very decided.

All the men looked aghast and gaped at Evangeline and began to assume various postures of collapse.

"Surely," ventured Napoleon, "there could be a symbolic taking."

Evangeline smiled. She was seeing the fun of the situation.

"Then you will take just a small morsel," Alphonse pleaded.

"Well, I'll take just a little then, rather than have these men go hungry."

"Good," laughed Alphonse, "the ban is lifted."

He picked up the carving knife and began filling the plates.

Everyone roared with laughter; the jolly party was off to a good start.

Napoleon marveled at his brother. When Alphonse was in these jovial moods, everything that came along was turned into fun.

Chapter 11

ABOVE the table the kerosene lamp sputtered. One corner of the wick was jagged and a shapely half-moon in black began to form inside the glass chimney.

It was nearly time to open the meeting. Alphonse Desjardins looked down at the chairs. They were filling up. Almost one hundred persons had gathered already in the hall of La Société des Artisans on Eden Street in Lévis.

They were all classes, he could see, neighbors and friends. That was well, because anybody might need credit and especially working people. They were interested. Curious, perhaps, too! His talking in the neighborhood had pricked their attention, else they would not have turned out like this. Well, it was simple. Few saved regularly, and there were few but that someday would need credit. Put these two facts together and what have you? Why, an organization!

What could he tell them now in speaking before them together?

Alphonse looked down at the people. They sat polite and expectant. Every man was a live question mark. Everyone was a potential accuser if something went wrong.

People make thrift. They save money here and there—in a sock, in a bag, or a bank. Little sums all scattered around, each apart from the other. God in Heaven! What would the St. Lawrence be if those drips of water were separated and scattered all over the mountains? No power, no flow, no drive, no source. The people's credit was like that. In pigeonholes.

Not all of it. Worse than that. Some persons saved money and put it in the hands of others to use. Thrift was a virtue. But that way its use was scattered about, too, just like the drops. Well, there was another way and neighbors who knew each other's honesty could work it.

He'd tell them. He was willing to take the risk of this experiment. An organization should be set up. It could begin to operate as a people's bank. A *caisse populaire*, they could call it.

He had drawn up by-laws upon which it could be run. It was a combination of features that had proved successful in credit societies started in Europe.

All the words that he was going to say came in torrents through his mind and dammed themselves up at the edge of his lips. When his name was called to speak to the meeting the words moved out, one driving the other to the ears before him. Alphonse did not trust oratory. He spoke simply. The years of his study poured out of him and created confidence.

Thrift, first of all, he told them. Even ten cents at a time. Then, in time, loans would be possible. This society must have a board of directors, a credit committee to look after loans, and a supervising committee to keep check on the activities of all.

The kerosene fumes came down heavy in the hall. Outside the December night settled black and cold. The half-moon on the lamp covered one side of the chimney when Alphonse sat down.

There was a lull, then clapping.

The people shuffled their feet and looked at each other. A clearing of throats set in and relayed around the hall.

What was going to happen next?

The crowd was grappling with its own reflexes.

This man Alphonse Desjardins had an idea. If he was taking the risk, that was very kind . . .

Alphonse didn't have long to wait. He found himself elected

president, after some small speeches by members brought on a successful vote for organization. They elected directors, as he had explained to them, and committees. The meeting was excited over this.

Alphonse made a signal for attention.

Would those who wished to subscribe shares in *La Caisse Populaire de Lévis* declare themselves?

A bunch of people came up. About eighty persons. They could sign the charter.

One was Abbé G. E. Carrier, head of the College of Lévis. That was good. Alphonse knew why. There was a cell of social studies at the College. Another was Abbé F. X. Gosselin, Curé of Lévis. That was support, too. The people respected them.

When the meeting was over and Alphonse went to his house his feelings were mixed. He was pleased to see these people band together to do something. It was exciting. People in action like that.

He was afraid, too. What might the future bring? That action could run off the track.

"Oh, I'm proud," Dorimène said when he told her of the meeting. "Proud that they trust you. They must, you know, when they make an organization like that. It is a salute to your idea and your studying."

Then suddenly he saw the worry and perplexity come into her eyes and she was saying: "I only hope that this will not lead into any trouble for you. You are a civil servant. And your name before the public . . ."

Alphonse took off his coat and hung his winter cap above it. He was afraid, too.

"We must pray," he said, hardly above a whisper.

Alphonse went to his room; right now he wanted privacy. He took a small tablet from the bureau. A few days before he had thought that he must write this prayer.

Yes, Dorimène was right. He was a civil servant. He worked

for the government. And here he was setting out to stir up the people to build their own credit system. He could still see the faces of the audience that had been before him that evening. Some faces had gaped at the thought that with the money spent on alcohol and tobacco they could build banks and own them. They had been startled. That might run to something yet.

As a civil servant you had to watch your p's and q's. You were a servant of government policy. You weren't supposed to have a reform plan of your own inside His Majesty's Canadian Government. That's what Parliament was for, to make policy. Why, any bunch with enough influence that looked sour at your ideas could have you investigated, you and all your doings. If things looked bad you could lose your job. He'd already been bounced once at Quebec. Alphonse laid the little tablet on the table and picked up his pen. He sat very still for a while. Dorimène came in, complained a little, and went to bed and slept. Still he sat there, unmoving. Now and then he put another paragraph on the little sheet. And silence reigned long in the graceful white house at the corner of Guenette and Blanchet Streets in Lévis.

On Sunday Alphonse went to High Mass, at Notre Dame de Lévis. Abbé Gosselin came out to preach.

It was the end of the nineteenth century, he said. At such a time it was in order to review the events of the past century and see what movements were casting light for the new century that was just to begin.

One of these, he went on, was the institution of the St. Vincent de Paul societies, because the condition of the working classes was the question of the hour. . . .

Alphonse opened his ears. Abbé Gosselin was on the edge of something. Alphonse sat back in his pew and waited for the shot he sensed was coming. The Abbé had been at the meeting.

"The century has seen being born those admirable works of Christian charity, known under the name of the St. Vincent de Paul societies, coming to the help of the needy. These associations and people's banks spread in Europe and gave substantial benefits to the population.

"In passing, I salute with deep satisfaction the foundation in our city of a similar society, or people's bank, giving promise of much benefit among you. I am proud to say it, that it will be to the glory of Lévis to have started the first people's bank on the Continent, and I wish it success and the very great popularity which is enjoyed by its sister organizations in Europe."

What a surprise! The parish priest coming out like that.

"I could hardly believe my ears," Alphonse told Dorimène at the dinner table. "I never expected such a recommendation among my fellow citizens. And so soon!"

Dorimène was silent now.

Three weeks later *La Caisse Populaire de Lévis* opened its doors for the first time.

The first deposit was ten cents. At the end of that first opening the total sum on hand was $26.40.

But a wheel had been unbraked in the community. A slow wheel it is true. Slowly it began to turn.

Alphonse was away to the sessions in the winter and home in the summer. Then he would jack things up and interest would be renewed. Money came in.

In the winters Dorimène was saddled with the whole burden. Year by year it grew. Her house had become like a public institution.

Rumor spread that Alphonse Desjardins was getting in deep.

Forty thousand dollars. It smells of something, that!

And there came the day when Dorimène could stand it no longer. Alphonse must be rescued from his dreams.

Chapter 12

It was not often that Dorimène took a trip. She was too busy with her family for that—even before the affairs of the *caisse populaire* had overburdened her household.

The eight-hour trip from Quebec to Ottawa did little to allay her fears. Sitting in the coach, she had ample time to rehearse in her mind all the reasons why the step Alphonse had taken was an unwise one. The more she thought of it, the more convinced she became.

The *caisse*! It was not something that one could finish and have done with. The more loans there were, the more involved it became; the more money you took in deposits, the bigger the business got; the more work and worry you had, the worse off you were.

Clearly the whole thing was an octopus, something to be shunned or put to an end. Already it had gone too far. And her husband must be saved from the consequences of his rash dream to help every Tom, Dick, and Harry.

Arrived in Ottawa, she went at once to her husband's quarters. She made herself known to his landlady and waited. It was evening and Alphonse would soon be in.

"Dorimène," he cried when he saw her. "Why, what brings you here?"

"The *caisse*, Alphonse," she said. "You must know it has become impossible."

"But why?"

"Why? They're coming all the time. Always someone is at the door."

Alphonse looked startled. "Sit down, dear," he said. "Sit down."

"I will not sit down," she said, sitting down.

"You are here at your work," she continued, a tone of reproach quavering in her voice. "I—I am in our house. They come, and they come. Knock, knock, knock all the time upon the door! They bring their money, some small, some much. Too much! They make deposits. They take out shares. They want loans. Lately, it is worse and worse. It can't go on, I tell you. It can't . . ."

Her voice that had been a sob had risen almost to a scream.

"My dear, it has been too much," he said, trying to soothe her, "too much. You need a rest, a change." Then he added quickly as an afterthought: "I will be home soon, you know, when the session ends. And I will take care of all that."

"No, Alphonse, it is not that. It is not for my own sake that I have come here."

"No? It is something else then?"

"It is not the bother and the worry of the *caisse* alone," she insisted. "It is that you are making a big mistake in your whole idea," she blurted, hating herself for hurting him.

Alphonse's head was lowered. He said quietly: "Time will tell—and I am not afraid."

"We are not bankers," she said, returning to the attack. "Why are we trying to be bankers? We are just people like everyone else. Why don't we be like everyone else and just work for the family that's growing up?"

"Work for the family? Well, of course, Dorimène. What am I doing here, but that! The *caisse*—that is for the people. We have known what the poor suffer; let us not forget it in our own fears."

"You give your time to that. What do you get out of it? What does the family get out of it? What will they ever get out of it, at best?"

"When it helps those who need help, we may not measure what the reward is."

"Yes, but what about if it fails? What if all the loans aren't paid? You will have to make it good; you know that; you said it in your letter."

"I do not see that any such thing is going to happen."

"Just the same, I'm afraid that it might happen, Alphonse. It would mean a blot on your name. And as for the children, what would they have?"

"But, my dear, it is too dark a view you are taking."

"We must think of these things, I tell you; we must think of our future and that of the children and our old age. Why, we might even lose the house that we struggled for years to own."

Dorimène, flushed and vehement, argued in defense of her home.

Alphonse said: "Come, come, we must eat. You are tired from the train."

They went to the nearby restaurant and ate among the civil servants. It was not a place for close talk. When they returned to his sitting room, a small fire was burning in the grate. They sat before it to talk.

"You, yourself, have said," she resumed, "that there is no law to protect the *caisse*. In case of loss, or failure, all the trouble will be laid at your doorstep."

"It is true. There is no law—as yet. When there is a law, the loss that could come to any one individual would be quite limited."

"And when will there be such a law?"

"When there is enough demand for the establishment of *caisses* to make our government see that such a law is needed. Until that time——"

"You and I will carry on with the load and the risks. Isn't that what you are saying?" she interrupted him.

He listened patiently to his wife. He could not reproach her; in some ways she was right.

"If we can hold on a little longer, things will look better," he said pleadingly.

"If," she scoffed. "That other one has opened up at St. Malo. I suppose Monsieur Alphonse Desjardins will be responsible for that one, too. Things are getting worse, it seems to me."

"They'll have to be careful about giving loans until there's a law, that's all."

"Even so. Think of the work and worry you'll have. And if one starts up, there might be another—and another. Where will it all end?"

"If we arouse the interest of good people, influential people, they could carry it on."

"Good people! Why, Alphonse, do you know what people are saying about you today in Lévis? They say you are a crackpot. Some say it is a hobby you have. A hobby with other people's money. Ha, ha! *Chacun a sa marotte*. But when it is with other people's money, why, that might be costly, indeed!"

Alphonse writhed but remained silent. He was more than a little curious to hear what his critics were saying. It hurt him to hear it from Dorimène but he would hear it all.

"Others are saying that you are only a dreamer of dreams," she went on. "A builder of castles in Spain—which are sure to come tumbling down. Others are saying that you are just a bore, always harping on one idea."

"When I started this work," he said, "I made up my mind that I wouldn't be turned aside by the gossip of those who didn't know any better."

"They say, too, that if Monsieur Desjardins knows so much about banking, why is it that he remains poor with only the small income of a civil servant? If he's so good in these questions of finance and economics, why is it that he doesn't make some money?"

Alphonse stood up. He was pale. It made his great eyes look larger in his head. His shoulders sagged.

"Humph!" she scoffed, looking up at him with fiery hauteur. "Making a slave of his wife to keep the *caisse*, and himself away all the time! They say that, too. Oh, yes, I get it good."

"Is there nothing that they do not say?" Alphonse wanted her to get all the taunts off her mind.

"They say definitely that you are also a fool," she replied. "What you have done, it cannot possibly succeed. Sooner or later when you are working with others, there is trouble. You are sure to lose. When that comes, our children will be on the street and will be condemned to utter poverty."

"Is that all?" he asked, and stared into the fire. It was as if he suddenly was far away and had a sanctuary somewhere within him from all critics.

"Now," she said, "I have told you."

"Let it go. Let it go. If they say I am a fool, what of it? That folly is my choice. I have dreamed to be useful to my fellow men."

Even in his dejection there was a wistful dignity she could not fathom.

They were silent then for a little time. She had come up against that streak of the mystical in Alphonse Desjardins—and how could it be coped with? How could anyone cope with it, knowing his stubbornness? Besides, she did not want to hurt him more than was necessary to warn him.

As for Alphonse he knew well that the fate of his plan depended upon what the people did with it. If they accepted the idea and built their *caisses populaires*, they could have the advantages. If they did not, all would fail and he would be remembered only as a fool. That was the risk he was taking.

For himself he did not care. But when it came to seeing his beloved wife so worried that she would reproach him and try to make him foresee their children reduced to poverty, it was too much. A sadness came over him such as he had not known since the days of his illness.

It had grown late in the night. The coals upon the hearth dimmed. The noises had died down on the street. When he raised his eyes to Dorimène he saw that her face was drawn. Her eyes held an anguish of anxiety. That was like a stab as he reflected what was the cause of it.

Had he, indeed, made a mistake?

Had he thought well enough about his work before he had started it?

How could he have foreseen all these entangling developments?

Tired though they were they talked on and on.

Dorimène summarized it all again: "We started a bank in our own house to help the people. Now we're in a predicament ourselves. Isn't it absurd? Please, let's close it now, before we get in deeper and deeper."

"Let's not do anything rash," he said. "Rather let us wait and get advice. After all, there are others. The priests of Lévis were for this from the start. Remember?"

He went on earnestly: "We could spoil a good work by a nervous measure now. Let's wait and hope for guidance. Let's sleep on it. *La nuit porte conseil. . . .*"

For the *Hansard* reporter of the Commons there was small hope of peace of mind that night. But by the next day he had decided upon a plan which he hoped would quiet the fears of his good wife.

Before she left for home, he said to her: "What do you think of the idea of placing the whole question before the Archbishop of Quebec, Monseigneur Bégin? He is well known in Lévis."

Dorimène was thoughtful for a moment. She knew well the great name of Monseigneur Bégin in Lévis and beyond. His word on anything would quash a horde of little gossipers.

"But could he be made to understand all the pitfalls?" she asked.

"I tell you what," Alphonse cried. "You will come and we will both go to him as soon as I return to Lévis. You will tell him all your objections and put it clearly before him."

"But will he listen? Will he understand?"

"He will listen. And you know well his reputation for clear-sightedness and good judgment. You can make him understand, I'm sure."

"And what then?"

"You will tell him all your worries. And we will abide by his decision. I promise you that."

"If he then says to stop now?"

"We will stop now. We will close the *caisse*."

"And if he says to keep on?" she asked.

"We will keep on."

In the end Dorimène accepted the idea.

It was time for Alphonse to go to his work, so Napoleon had come to see her to the station.

"You know, of course, what brought me to Ottawa," she told him as they entered the train gate.

"The *caisse populaire*. It is a worry on you?"

"Beyond that. It will ruin us, I'm afraid."

"Well, I've cautioned him, too, Dorimène. But he will go on. He has developed in these years since his illness a habit of mind. It is a slow activity that never rushes and never stops. They say that men like that are dangerous. To themselves, I mean. But, well . . . who knows? He has a great faith in that work."

"Dangerous for sure! But not only for himself. There is the family to be thought of."

"What, then, are you to do, Dorimène?"

"We are going to place the whole matter before Archbishop Bégin as soon as Alphonse comes home. I, too, will go and speak my mind! I hope Archbishop Bégin will put his foot down on the whole business. It's not a light matter, the breaking up of a home!"

"Dorimène!" There was incredulity in his voice.

The bell clanged and the "on board" sounded.

Dorimène shook her head sadly from side to side and climbed aboard.

Chapter 13

ALPHONSE went as usual to his desk in the House of Commons. For once he was glad to be there. In a way it was a refuge from the anxieties fanned up by the events of the previous evening. Though Dorimène herself had left for Lévis, the implication of her words remained with him, and in fact became all the keener with her absence.

Had she, too, turned against him because of the *caisse populaire*?

That thought followed him; and all the way from his apartment to the door of the Commons, his heart was heavy with it.

Once he slid into his chair at his desk it was different. He opened his notebook and made ready his pencils. All else must be excluded from the mind. Fourteen sessions of recording the debates in shorthand had taught him that. When the words came thick and fast from the members you had no time to think of anything else.

But when his "take" was over and finally the House adjourned for the day and he returned to the quiet of his apartment, all Dorimène's arguments came back to him.

He was alone now. On the very spot where they had had the argument he could think more deliberately upon the information she had given him. She had told him what others thought of him; he still winced under the slash of her words. It had been painful. Yet it was in a way interesting. Not everyone had revealed to them what others thought of them. At any rate he knew now where he stood with certain of his neighbors.

In their minds he was a dreamer. He reflected on this a little grimly, sitting appropriately quiet in the twilight as the noises of the city died down and shadows deepened between the lamp-posts.

To them he was a dreamer of idle dreams, a builder of castles in Spain—things that came tumbling down, given a little time. He was a sort of modern Don Quixote, tilting at that most fabulous of windmills—the lack of credit for those who needed credit most. Tilting at poverty! That's what it was—for if you had means you could get all the credit you needed.

He was a crackpot. He had chosen for himself the hobby of collecting other people's money and putting it in a thing he called a *caisse populaire*.

He was a bore. He always came around to the same theme—his pet idea. He was the sort of fellow you dodged when you saw him coming.

He tried to read a while but gave that up. He started to prepare for bed.

It was not pleasant, either, to realize that your friends thought you something of a poseur, a faker. According to them, if a man knew something about banking and credit and such, there was only one thing for him to do: make some money for himself. It was quite simple. This Alphonse Desjardins was only pretending.

He looked at his reflection in the mirror. Was this really the face of a fool? Many of his friends now thought so.

One of these days the *caisse* would go crashing to the wall. The depositors would sue for their losses and the whole thing would be a reproach to the name of Desjardins forever. They would lose their home and the children would be on the street.

"What a shame!" He could hear the scorn in the voices of his accusers. Poor Mrs. Desjardins, to be put through an experience like that!

At last he got into bed. He could not sleep.

In the loneliness of the night these thoughts kept repeating themselves in his mind hour after hour. At times they almost made him feel guilty, for he could see that his critics believed them true.

Were they, after all, right and he wrong?

He could hear their mocking voices. He knew the types they were. They were men who had grown up in a business environment and had never thought to challenge its ethics. They accepted that environment and made whatever they could out of whatever came to hand. They were entirely innocent of any social thinking whatever. They accepted life as a nasty, dog-eat-dog business and did not want to give that up so long as they could be the eating dogs and not the eaten. The letter to the world by Pope Leo XIII calling on all men, fourteen years before, to learn a just economic code, had left them cold—Catholic and churchgoing though they were. They followed economic codes that were born outside the Church, and now all were tied down alike in a race for material goods.

They were not bad men. They were the children of an age.

They had slipped back to accepting, as their first principle of economic conduct, "I am not my brother's keeper." That was the principle of the first murderer. It was these who upheld in everyday form the denial of the brotherhood of man, and who therefore lived in a state of undercover rebellion and in perpetual deeds of treason against the Fatherhood of God.

No; they could not be right. They were blind, and had not been stirred from their blindness.

Thus were his thoughts at dawn.

He recalled the prayer that he had written and put away when he had first decided to start the *caisse populaire*. He had asked then for light as to whether he was doing the right thing.

He would put all his faith in it. Let them mock and jeer to their heart's content. He would go ahead.

Chapter 14

IN FAIRNESS to Dorimène it must be said that Alphonse had had access to sources and convictions which she did not have. This was through certain of the professors at the College of Lévis, the gray granite buildings of which loomed in the background just opposite the Desjardins' home. In truth Dorimène was at a disadvantage. Busy with her home and her children, she did not have all his opportunities for study.

A little group had formed a cell of social studies. They had met from time to time in round-table discussions in the room of one of the priests.

There were three professors in particular who were taking part. There was Abbé Joseph Hallé, the philosopher of the group. He later became Bishop of Hearst, in Ontario. There was Abbé Stanislas Irénée Lecours, bursar of the College, who introduced the *caisse* among the students and the other professors. There was the young Abbé Philibert Grondin. And there was Alphonse.

From time to time, they would meet at night. They would sit talking under fuming little lamps. They were trying to clarify their thought, trying to foresee all sides of the problem of getting the common people to organize a credit system for themselves out of their own savings.

Alphonse wanted these meetings. He wanted the idea discussed to see how well it would stand up. He wanted to be ready. For he knew that any effort to get the people to manage their own money and credit even in a small way would be looked upon with suspicion. It would be attacked from influential heights. It would be called socialism for a smear.

What Alphonse especially wanted to hear argued out was the philosophical and moral justification of organizing the people, just the common little people, those who go by the name of "the poor." At that time, it should be remembered, the right of assembly and organization of the working class was not as well understood as it is today.

"Is it that only a certain very few people are, as it were, predestined to handle the money of a community?" he asked at a memorable session held one night in the previous October. "Who ever stops to think what power is placed into the hands of these few when that is done? And they do not ask us to do it. It's rather the other way round: we ask them to take our money and keep it for us. We do not realize that when we do that we place control of the funds of credit outside our own hands. Why do we do that?"

"It is doubtless due," said Abbé Hallé, "to the fact that little or no thought has been put on the subject. With the rise of capitalism the old social organization of the villages tended to go to pieces. Individualism arose as the way of economic conduct. That meant that everyone went out for himself."

"It is not then a case of a few being born to this service; it is that they went into this service because there was no one else doing it." The speaker was Philibert Grondin, the young professor, whose face was quickly aglow at any thought of assisting the people. He was a man of medium height, humorous and unassuming, quick and animated in his movements, and ideas swept his face like rays of light.

"There is, of course, a very real question of competence," said Abbé Lecours, the fourth member of the group. "Taking care of money, keeping accounts, and, above all, looking after loans—that takes experience. A few mistakes and the whole thing gets discredited."

Abbé Lecours was for putting the weak points, though he was just as much for the *caisse* as the others. In this they were all agreed. It was very useful to bring out the weak points, and some one of the group always took that side to make things clearer and to have knowledge of the objections that might be encountered.

"My idea," said Alphonse, "is that it all depends on thrift. If the savings are made by the people and the funds accumulated, the competence to manage and handle that will soon follow, or will soon be found."

"You mean someone will get interested in that type of work when the idea is known?" asked Abbé Grondin.

"Exactly. I look at it this way. Do those fortunate few people who inherit money know how to manage it? In most cases, no. What happens? Why, the estate is put under the management of someone who knows what to do. But the heirs get the benefits. I ask, why cannot the same be done with a people's estate in the field of credit?"

A current of excitement ran through the other three at Alphonse's words. A wave of eagerness banded them together under the fuming little lamps that cast dim shadows upon the row of bookshelves that lined the walls.

"The first thing," Alphonse went on, "is to teach the people to save, and to put their savings together. Once a considerable amount has been brought together, I'm sure that someone to manage it in the interests of the people can be found, having in mind, of course, that there will be always a board of directors and committeemen. Then, too, they'll learn as they go along."

"Do you think our people can be taught to save in a way that would make it worth while?" asked Abbé Lecours.

"Why, if families only but saved in a *caisse populaire* what they habitually waste in liquor, tobacco, and not a few useless commodities, they would soon accumulate a ready source of credit," said Abbé Grondin.

"There is no doubt about it— if they but would," said Abbé Hallé.

"Since they have done this in Belgium and Germany and

Italy, why cannot we do it here?" asked Alphonse. "If some of our people, even the poor, are wasteful, it is because of a kind of despair of ever getting anywhere. There has been no organization whatever in the community to teach them thrift and the use of their own credit."

"Just think what a defect that is! The building and use of credit is a vital function in making a living. The poorer the man, the more vital it is. Yet all that has been left to chance." Abbé Grondin was speaking with more than his usual animation.

Alphonse settled himself in his chair. He was a heavy man again now, though not as fleshy as before his long illness.

"I am sure of this," he said. "Without the *caisse populaire* our people cannot be freed from the yoke of foreign capitalists and that of our own usurers."

"That is a very big job," laughed Abbé Lecours. He spoke with the realism of the bursar's office.

"And all the more reason why it should be tackled," said Abbé Grondin. "The longer it is left, the worse will become the condition of the people."

"I have my own view regarding the practical side," said Alphonse. "Anyhow we are getting our experience in that now. You all know of the success of our first *caisse* in these few years. From the standpoint of savings it is very good. There is no doubt that this thing can be done and an equal success can be achieved in other communities in time. The one question is, Are we on sound moral grounds in presuming to organize the people in this way? Could it be that our religious or civil leaders might find a legitimate objection?"

Abbé Lecours flexed his brows before he spoke. "The civil leaders," he said, "would have to be convinced. As for the religious, well, Abbé Hallé, what do you think?"

"Workingmen's associations and all their rights are defended strongly," replied the Abbé, "in the encyclical Rerum Novarum, by Pope Leo XIII. A question that might be raised by some is, Is the *caisse populaire* a workingmen's association?"

"Why not? What else is it?" Abbé Grondin was emphatic.

"It certainly is for welfare purposes and in the deepest sense," added Alphonse.

"All right," replied Abbé Hallé. "As long as the purpose of your societies is just and good there can be no question, morally speaking, of the right of the people to band together. That is a natural right, banding together, and the state or civil authorities cannot take it away unless the intention is known to be harmful."

"That right has not been understood by the people generally," said Abbé Lecours. "As a matter of fact few have ever thought of it."

"There is," went on Abbé Hallé, speaking now in the tones of a teacher and philosopher who is on familiar ground, "the right of assembly, of association, the right to form corporate bodies within the state. That cannot be taken away. The rich and the entrepreneurs have always understood it and used it. They have their corporations. The purpose of these is, most often, to make money."

"A *caisse populaire*," exclaimed Alphonse, "is a co-operative society for credit. Its purpose is service. That fact should help to make its right all the more secure."

"These are high ideals. For service? Don't forget that many will be skeptical about all that." It was Abbé Lecours with a note of warning.

"But on the other hand," suggested Abbé Grondin, "will not the *caisse* be accepted for what it does? If it builds up a social fund in the parish, if it inspires people to save, if the needy are now able to get loans when before they couldn't, all that in time should answer the critics."

"A job must be done of making the advantages known," said Alphonse. "That is one of the biggest jobs—reaching the people and getting them started."

"With talking this subject out it becomes clearer," said Abbé Hallé. "The more one thinks on it the better it looks. I'm thinking in particular of your emphasis on thrift, Alphonse. If one preaches thrift just to individuals one is liable to make misers. You know there are men mean with their families and who want to keep their money in a sock. But thrift as it will be taught through the *caisse* will not be miserliness and hoarding. There will be saving, but it will be social saving, social thrift. There will be both a saving and a giving away because one's savings go into a pool to help one's fellows. In this one act, then, there is a double virtue."

"You think then," and Abbé Lecours leveled a glance at the speaker whose analysis had struck all of them, "that there should not be forthcoming any objections from moral and philosophical sources, which sometime in the future, let us say, might embarrass the proponents of such a scheme?"

Abbé Hallé responded quickly: "I can't foresee the slightest grounds for any such objections. The very opposite is what I would hope for."

"*Bon,*" cried Abbé Lecours, well pleased to be bested in his role of putting the weak points.

"It is understood, of course," continued Abbé Hallé, "that people organized in *caisses populaires* will stick to the business of credit and not get tangled up with other ideas that could drag them onto dangerous ground."

Abbé Grondin raised both hands: "We must have," he said, "a clear explanation of what the *caisse populaire* is and how it works. That is very necessary."

Without any delay Alphonse replied: "I have in mind the main points. They are drawn from the record of such societies in Europe as well as from the experience that we have had in our first *caisse populaire* here in Lévis. I have even written these main points down, and if you are so minded, gentlemen, I shall be glad to run through them."

"Go on." The three priests concurred. They were used to

burning the midnight oil when Alphonse Desjardins came to their rooms in those days to talk about the need of a system of credit.

Alphonse looked at his three companions one after the other. He saw that they eagerly awaited his words and then he launched into his description:

"The idea of the *caisse populaire* is new in this country. It is a co-operative association for savings and loans and it is capable of variability in amounts of capital and also in membership. It is not, then, a simple accumulation of capital.

"Consider its use in a community. All those who have experienced the same economic wants join together and accept a program large and well defined. It must be perfectly understood and carefully carried out. Without these fundamental conditions, it is impossible to expect success, or even to conceive of it.

"This is, above all, a union of persons. In such a setup, the capital is only a simple tool. It is the slave instead of being the master, as it is among other types of organization, for example, the ordinary joint-stock company. Capital has not the directing power, as is the case in the financial concentrations so much in vogue now and which have for their object the increase of profits at the expense of unorganized capital, or of other economic forces.

"Just as the capitalistic companies have to have some rules to guide them, in the same way this association of persons ought also to have by-laws to guide its operations.

"The first and most important point will have to do with the choice of those who will be members. The conditions of admission ought to be such that each can fulfill them. Then as each demonstrates his spirit of co-operation, his honesty, love of work, and the practice of making even small savings, one feels that nearly everybody can fulfill these conditions."

Alphonse paused for breath. No need to question the look of interest on the faces of his hearers. He wet his lips with his tongue and went on.

"Now as to the purposes of such a society. There are two principal ones. The first will be to encourage thrift in the form of regular savings. These are to be encouraged even if they are very small—for the poorest people are the ones who need this most. As we shall see——"

Abbé Hallé broke in: "This is going to be a job of serious teaching, to get the people to understand that."

"But," interjected Abbé Grondin, "it is a subject of prime interest. Most of our people are poor. They must be interested in fighting their poverty. Here is one way to do it. That is what this is—a battle against poverty!"

Abbé Lecours uncrossed his legs. He remained silent.

"The second purpose," continued Alphonse, "is made possible by the first. It is to extend loans to those of the membership who need them. This service is extended to members only. The reason for the loan will be known and repayments will be agreed upon on a regular plan.

"In order to make sure of the best possible choice of members, the field of each society must be defined with great care. This is to be done on a territorial or occupational basis. It must be remembered that the *caisse populaire* is to function amongst the most humble of our people. And they are to be based on the principle of one man, one vote. In this plan the persons know each other well. It would not be so if the scope went beyond, for example, the parish."

Abbé Lecours raised a questioning hand. He had been thinking of Abbé Grondin's words about fighting poverty.

"Can the poor help the poor?" he asked. "What can they save? It is nothing, it seems to me. Could you get them even to try?"

Alphonse swallowed. Did Abbé Lecours think the *caisse populaire* an impractical dream? Had the rumor "crackpot" reached him too and made its mark? Did he think all this business of helping the poor a grandiose notion? Were the poor, after all, something that grew and grew like weeds, and you could do nothing but make your way among them with as little contact and as little thought as possible?

But no. The question was a legitimate one.

"I think so," he said evenly. "They can save a little. It only takes a little saved when they can get a loan. And make a little more. That is being taught the use of credit.

"Besides," he continued, and the force of his words startled the priests, "*much of the poverty we see has its root in despair.* They give up trying. They think they will always be failures, and become more wasteful than the rich. They go down and down. If we profess Christian brotherhood we can hope to arouse them from that. Here is one way to start."

Before he had time to finish, Abbé Grondin was chafing to seize the thread of the subject: "In some countries," he began, "religion was not supposed to be concerned with the condition of the working masses. The capitalists must have free rein. *Laissez faire!* Humph! That was never so in the Province of Quebec. Our first Bishop, the venerable Laval, had teachers of the arts and crafts brought here so that the common people might by their work provide themselves with the necessities. If the Church worked with a feudal system here, it was because it hoped to inspire the seigneurs to do the right thing by the people. Now that has passed and capitalism has come. The poor are still with us. It is rather worse now for those who don't succeed, for capitalism has taught the people not to employ themselves at crafts but to find an employer. They leave our farms and villages and seek wages.

"I tell you if we do not attack the problem of poverty, the state of the masses sunk in poverty, will we be doing right? Can we preach patience, and Christ crucified to them, when we ourselves are well cared for and the cross is on them to a backbreaking degree?

"The doctrine of the cross is not exhorting the other fellow to bear, it is helping him—like the Samaritan.

"The man who says to another who is suffering and in great want of this world's goods, 'Bear your Cross. God will help,' and at the same time doesn't do anything practical himself to help the sufferer is a liar and a betrayer of God. God has ordained no other way that a man can be helped but by another of his kind."

"You would say, then, Abbé Grondin, that these reforms that Alphonse is undertaking are in the nature of charity?" It was Abbé Lecour's question.

"They would be that, too."

"In the nature of justice also," said Abbé Hallé. "The people have a right to organize their own economy if they are able. The fact that they have been letting capitalists and outsiders do it for them doesn't take away the right. If they can learn to work together it will be their salvation in an economic sense."

"If they start in the field of credit, they may branch later into other fields of economy," said Alphonse. "It will do two things: teach them to work together and give them the funds to go into other group enterprises."

The four men drew closer in their talk. Discussion across the table grew animated. The night deepened. The little lamps sputtered and fumed as the wicks burned down and etched jagged vignettes of flame inside their smoky chimneys.

The hearts of all four were dedicated to humanity. And as they talked, they mutually inspired each other.

There was a noise in the corridor. Abbé Lecours excused himself—obviously on an errand of discipline. One of the college boys had stolen out and was now winning his way back step by step.

The three men were silent for a few moments. Alphonse permitted his mind to wander in reverie.

Across the river the lights of Quebec threw vaster shapes of flame upon the black earth. The Château Frontenac cut the sky line high with its many spires above the Dufferin Terrace. There stood the statue of Samuel de Champlain, the great discoverer, his plumed hat in one hand, his titles to the land in another. He stood as one enthralled and offering his followers the riches and liberty of a continent.

Here, too, men met and talked in the night—across tables, in homes, in taverns and barrooms. But it was not particularly to help the people. It was to make money, to make a career, to get ahead.

With businessmen, brought up in the rough and tumble of competition, with lawyers and doctors, with university graduates, schooled in ethics and philosophy, it was all the same code.

Make money and get ahead.

Their women demanded it.

The riches and liberty of a continent! The sight of it, Alphonse mused, had put that strange light in the eyes of Champlain and a God-like expectancy in his figure.

The Promised Land! Champlain had seen it in a hundred journeys of exploration, glistening there through the fierce dangers of the wilderness—the Great Lakes and waterways, the intervale lands, the valleys, the hills, the plains and the mountains, the vast old stands of timber, the schools of fishes and the fowls, the fur-bearing animals, the buffalo, the riches in the soil and under the soil—all the great harvest that the Almighty had farmed up and ripened in America through a thousand ages.

And for whom was it, this Promised Land? Why, it could be for none other than those humble enough to work it and virile enough to people it. For workpeople! None other, obviously. For the woodsmen and farmers and fishermen. For the outcasts of Europe, men who had learned valor fighting the tyranny of kings, refugees of a social order too rigid, too barren of soul to admit the right of life in all men.

None but they could have conquered this Promised Land. But as the generations came and went, the men who thought only of money came to dominate. Now the riches and liberty of a continent were being thrown into their hands.

A new frontier must be broken. The humble people must be taught how to control some of the wealth they created, that was clear.

Abbé Lecours came in and slammed the door. It aroused Alphonse from his reverie.

Then he went on with his explanation of what the *caisse populaire* would be and could be if it got the acceptance of the people and their leaders. Now and then the priests interrupted and engaged in questions and discussion on their own.

They were excited. The French-Canadian people could build a savings and credit system of their own. They had been traditionally on the short end of money handling, these "habitants." These were a land and craft people, carefree and full of song, while the English had mastered the art of money-handling.

Well, Alphonse Desjardins had something. Above all, he was practical. Though a great dreamer, too, he could turn around and be as practical as any huckster.

He emphasized above all that the *caisse populaire* was to be an association of persons. This he insisted over and over. No matter how many shares a person had he could only have one vote.

Le suffrage a pour unique base la personne!

As the business was controlled by the general assembly of members, or the annual meeting, as it was called, this was very important. The value of a share was to be low enough to permit the poorest to have one. It was to be five dollars and could be bought by weekly payments of ten cents each. It was amazing how even the poorest families could build themselves a credit bank if they got the idea and really stuck to it.

He introduced the term *social capital*. He told about the policy on loans that could be safely instituted, and of rates of interest to be charged; the money thus earned would be rebated after costs of operation were taken care of.

Abbé Hallé said that there was real hope in such a plan if a lot of societies should come into being. In time they would all add up to make a great force against poverty. It was poverty, he said, that gave rise to communism. Years ago the Communists had stated their intentions in the Communist Manifesto. It would be a dictatorship in the name of the workers. France had been shaken more than once.

Abbé Grondin agreed. The man who understood well this coming menace, he said, was Frederic Ozanam of Paris, a great French writer. He had founded the St. Vincent de Paul societies —on the idea that every well-disposed Christian would want to do something to help those less fortunate than himself.

"When we find that great thinker believing firmly that it would be necessary to 'annihilate the political spirit to the advantage of the social spirit,' we begin to realize how well he foresaw the rise of political dictatorships in the name of the working masses."

"With such a premise to start with, he would hardly be well received at a party caucus," laughed Alphonse.

"It was needed, perhaps, to make an extreme statement to get attention. People have been for so long leaving all their problems to politicians to solve that they have forgotten that there is any way else." It was Abbé Hallé.

"Exactly," said Abbé Grondin. "They put themselves in the hands of a government. What is that? It is apt to be a group of politicians vying with each other for power. The worse the problems have been permitted to become, the more dangerous the power. For the common man it would be like getting walled up in concrete."

"Is it not being too hard on politicians, that view?" asked Abbé Lecours.

"Ozanam did not mean it in that way," replied Abbé Grondin. "He meant that the politician deserved to be rescued from too many problems. Arouse a new social spirit! What did that mean? It meant that the people should attack as many of their problems as possible locally in their own communities by a program of social organization to help solve their most pressing economic problem. That way the people can be united. Party politics, on the other hand, tends to divide them. In the long run, of course, we want the greatest possible concurrence between the social and the political."

"What more practical way to employ a social spirit than in having the people practice thrift and build a credit system together?" asked Alphonse.

To this they all agreed.

Abbé Grondin was looking in his pocket. "I would like to read this," he said. "It is by Ozanam and written in 1835, when he was twenty-two."

The other three listened closely while Abbé Grondin bent under one of the flickering lamps:

> The question which divides people today is not a question of political form, it is a social question; it is to know which will bring to it the spirit of egotism or the spirit of sacrifice, if society is to be a grand exploitation for the benefit of the strong or a consecration of each for the good of all—true co-operation, and especially for the protection of the weak.
>
> There are a great many people who have much and who wish to have more. There are many others who have not enough, who have nothing and who wish to take what others will give them.
>
> Between these two classes of men a struggle is rising, and that struggle promises to be terrible: on the one side the power of money, on the other the power of despair.
>
> Between these armed enemies, it is necessary that we throw ourselves, if not to stop them at least to lessen the shock. And our youthful age and our modest state makes the role of mediator easy as our name of Christian makes it obligatory.

When he had finished reading, Alphonse was the first to speak.

"It could have been written yesterday," he said. "It fits so well."

They resumed their discussion.

The more they talked about poverty, about economics and politics, the more sure they became that the *caisse populaire* would be a good thing if the people just took it up. By the time the meeting broke up, all were filled with the idea.

From such little gatherings Alphonse laid up in his mind a store of conviction that was to serve him well in his many controversies.

Chapter 15

THE train was getting near to Quebec City. The young priest arose from his seat. As he swayed in the aisle you could see how tall he was. His long arms hung down loosely in his cassock and his great hands looked like paddles as he went by the seats.

His stride was like that of the plowman, or the sailor—men who walk contemplatively in God's vastnesses and whose movement of body has come to be in beat with the rhythm of their environment. His face, though ascetic, had in its peace, more than usual strength, and a trace of that carefree brightness seen in those who put all their trust in God. He got off the train at Quebec, hailed a *calèche*, and told the driver to take him to the house of the Archbishop.

In a little time he was received by Louis Nazaire Bégin, Archbishop of Quebec. To him he had come to report on the state of his country parish and in particular to see his superior's approval upon the steps just taken in trying to bring to completion the village church which was to serve 130 farm families. This was uphill work. Soon the young priest waxed voluble upon his many difficulties.

"But be not discouraged," counseled the Archbishop. "An older pastor would be well pleased with what has already been accomplished. A church is not built in a day. A church is a citadel built against the enemies of humanity. It is not to be finished without a struggle. Expect that. Be patient."

"Your Grace," said the priest, "it is not only of the church, this building that is to be the house of God, that I am thinking. It is of the whole parish." He repeated: "The whole parish. Everyone."

Archbishop Bégin straightened in his chair. The severe black of his cassock was broken by a sash of purple at the waist. From his full, high forehead the hair had receded. His eyes were serious, but kindly. The faint tremor of a smile played on the clean-cut, decisive mouth.

"Just what do you mean?" he asked.

"Our people are very poor in Lac Saint André," replied the priest. "Very poor. They till the soil in spring and summer. In the winter they are in the woods, cutting timber for the companies that come from God knows where. Their families are large. Often there is not sufficient——"

"But my dear Father LeForte," broke in the Archbishop, "surely it is not news that people are poor. For the three hundred years that our race has been in this land, they have battled with poverty in the wilderness. Surely they have not lost the power to create wealth—at least certain of the essentials which they need."

"Pardon me, your Grace, if I say that the wealth which is created in our parish is not used by the people in our parish. Take the timber. An outside company owns the camps. Our men do the cuttings for a small wage; the lumber is taken away—while their own houses are small and cold. With the maple it is the same. In the spring the sap is gathered. It is taken away and made into sugar elsewhere. In the homes the children have no sweetening. It is the same with the cream and the cattle and lambs. Of these they must sell the best—and very often they starve themselves."

"Your statements are the fruit of not a little observation," said his Grace.

"The point I wish to make," went on the priest, "is that while our farms are well able to create wealth in many shapes, they seem to have lost the power of using it. A system has come to use it for them."

"Is there no capital available in your parish such as could start some enterprises essential to the people's welfare?"

"What money there is goes out of the parish in various ways, some of it in the form of payments on insurance policies. This goes to great financial organizations in distant cities. Year by year, the use of such funds is lost to the neighborhood."

"No doubt the people need guidance in economic affairs as well," the Archbishop said. "You are, Father, a discerning student of that science—also?"

The effect of the "also" was not lost. It mean that the priest's main science must always be that spiritual development by which his people would be led to their eternal home.

The young priest stood up to go. His figure was gaunt and his stride a little awkward. Here was a man not apt to get his worlds mixed up. Archbishop Bégin caught him by the shoulders and pushed him gently back into his chair.

"Please, please. I must hear more of your views. Tell me more about your parish."

"In my parish, people are born, grow up, and go away. It is the same with the wealth. What is produced there goes out. Life goes out of there. We export life. Our parish is a harvest for outside entrepreneurs. Must our people become road walkers and migrants in the land that their ancestors tamed? Simply because their worldly and alert fellow citizens have learned the secrets of controlling and managing business?"

They talked for an hour before the priest left the house.

An Archbishop of Quebec always has had plenty to think about. It has been so from the days of Laval—in whose name and memory a massive row of buildings abide.

What decisions of great moment have been mooted and counseled within this chancellery! In any century could be picked one or more that made history on the North American continent.

In 1757 peace with the British after the defeat of Montcalm. In 1776 rejection of an invitation from the American Colonies to join in war against the British. And what a difference that made. With Quebec in that war, the whole continent would be under the banner of the Republic. But the Quebec people never liked war. Any war left them cold.

Now was the beginning of the twentieth century. Other questions were in the air. There was the struggle between labor and capital, and the problem of the impoverishment of the working masses. Factories were coming in the cities. They employed men; they drew on the surplus manpower of the countryside. The wages they paid were low. The rural people who moved in and became dependent on this wage often sank into depths of great poverty.

Whereas in former times, on the land, they had produced many of their own essentials in food, by keeping cows, pigs, hens, and chickens, and growing wheat, oats, and vegetables, they now produced nothing whatever. With their tiny wage, they tried to live. There were rent, furniture, clothes—more clothes than in the country. Then there was food! The man worked long hours and needed good food. Every bite had to be bought from a store. Much of it was stale, secondhand, and diluted. And all out of that tiny wage. It just couldn't be done at all. No wonder, the Archbishop reflected sadly, that men fell into despair, became brutish and drunken, became wasteful and dissolute. By giving up their hold on land and by ceasing to practice the age-old sustaining crafts of the village and the homestead, they had become completely dependent upon the wage system. They were slaves of capital.

Men were born to work. Life had no meaning without work to do. Archbishop Bégin remembered well the passage in Scripture which said, "Thy work is thy portion." Yet now, in the twentieth century, aflame with the fire of invention and progress and blackened with the smoke of industrialization, the condition under which men were taught to work was only that capital needed a hired hand. This was less than human and could not last. It was not deliberately planned or willed but came about as a by-product of the dominance of capital and the ease with which it swayed the imaginations of the people with thoughts of money and endless novelty in the material creations of industry.

The Archbishop rummaged among the papers on his broad oak desk. The tall figure was slightly tense and the sensitive mouth reflected the mood of a student. There was, he felt, searching the while among his books, something diabolical in it all. It was called progress; and there were many time- and labor-saving conveniences that captivated all. Freedom from drudgery could be good. But what drudgery could equal not being wanted? This corroded and poisoned the souls of men. In former times there had been systems of frank slavery and the relationship of master and slave. It had had its abuse. But the slave often became so indispensable to the master that they grew attached to each other; even the slave became wanted and could feel proud of it. For the majority of wage workers it was not so. Their employment was a purely commercial transaction. Their labor was bought as if it were a chunk of matter. No wonder they became bitter and infected each other with a slow contagion. Wherever industrialism reared its chimneys to belch its smoke and cinders against the landscape, around that you could draw a circle, and in a few years' time there would be a moral and physical slum. Need it be so?

Was this the price to pay for a mode of production that tended to make people more materialistic in their desires, in their wants, habits, and ideas too? All stimuli came now to pinion them down to considerations of this life—which passed like an arrow shot into the air—and to blind them to all thoughts of the beckoning vastness of the life to come. For this Jesus Christ had given his life.

The world was making a poor bargain. Could the working class save itself from this morass?

Archbishop Bégin spied at last the book he wanted. It was a small book. Across its cover were the words *Rerum Novarum—on the Condition of the Working Masses.* He took it to a chair by the window where the light was good and settled himself to read.

From the walls looked down three hundred years of bishops. He read:

We have insisted that, since it is the end of Society to make men better, the chief good that Society can be possessed of is virtue. Nevertheless, in all well-constituted States it is a by no means unimportant matter to provide those bodily and external commodities the use of which is necessary to virtuous action. And in the provision of material well-being, the labor of the poor—the exercise of their skill and the employment of their strength in the culture of the land and the workshops of trade—is most efficacious and altogether indispensable. Indeed, their co-operation in this respect is so important that it may be truly said that it is only by the labor of the working man that States grow rich. . . .

The most important of all are Workman's Associations; for these virtually include all the rest. History attests what excellent results were affected by the Artificers' Guilds of a former day . . . such associations should be adapted to the requirements of the age in which we live—an age of greater instruction, of different customs and more numerous requirements in daily life. . . .

Let the State watch over these societies of citizens united together in the exercise of their right; but let it not thrust itself into their peculiar concerns and their organization, for things move and live by the soul within them, and they may be killed by the grasp of a hand from without.

His interest deepened; his attention grew fixed. Absorbed, the Archbishop read on—and on.

On Thursday morning of the next week the porter at the Archbishop's house announced callers. They were a man and his wife—Mr. and Mrs. Alphonse Desjardins of Lévis. Archbishop Bégin was always glad to see anyone from Lévis. It was his own home town, and though his life's work had taken him to other parts he had never forgotten it. The name Alphonse Desjardins above all awakened a quick response. As Bishop of Chicotimi, he had seen copies of the *Debates Desjardins*.

The two came slowly into the high-ceilinged room. Alphonse was at his ease. Years in the Parliament had given him poise in the presence of notables. Dorimène was flushed and halting. She was not used to this. In the presence of the Archbishop she floundered in a resurgence of youthful bashfulness that but served to set out her mature beauty in striking contrast. But she was soon rescued by the cordial welcome, as his Grace whisked them inside. They kissed his ring; then sat on staid chairs and gathered closely together. Soon the barriers between them were down.

Alphonse and Dorimène came quickly to the point of their visit. They had started a savings and loan society. It was mostly conducted from their own house. It was to teach people to save, but also to make loans available to the poor members. It would be owned and conducted by the members, who would elect competent officers, set the rate of interest, and other major policies.

Then they began to paint the difficulties that they met. Together they told of the attacks of their critics and the names that were being called.

Archbishop Bégin listened discreetly. He was known as a man who listened in silence to all sides in an argument, and then, if he had to make a decision, went to it directly.

Dorimène told of her great fear. It was that, quite apart from the burden of keeping all these accounts, there would some day be a loss through a bad loan or loans, or even a theft, and Alphonse Desjardins alone would have to foot the bill.

"What type of people do you contemplate as members?" asked the Archbishop.

"Only persons of known good character," replied Alphonse.

"And you have already during these few years, perhaps, gathered a small amount?"

"We have saved, since starting, forty thousand dollars."

"Forty thousand! Why you amaze me!"

"It is a very great care to be responsible for such a sum," said Dorimène.

"Well, yes, but think of your success. My dear Madame Desjardins, is it not your very success that is the cause of your complaint?" His Grace's smile was merry.

Alphonse sat speechless for the moment.

"My first thought is to congratulate you—both of you. Why, you have done what everyone said could not be done—taught a group of our people to save in a little bank of their own. Excellent. But I must hear more of this. Go on, go on."

The co-operative bank was something new. Alphonse launched into a complete description. The principle of it had been proven. The people could and would save, and could supply much of their own credit needs. So far he was responsible for any losses, as founder, but that would not continue to be so. There must certainly be a law under which the little banks would come and which would protect the members from loss. That was so in European countries. It could be made so here with influential support from proper authorities.

The little banks, Alphonse continued, owned and run by the people, would fill a gap in the parishes. There was really no economic organization in the parishes. The people either did not save or put their money in banks owned and run as branches of the big banks.

Dorimène interrupted now and then to put her views strongly: "We are, your Grace, but poor people. It is a big work that my husband is thinking of. He has put his life in it—reading and thinking and listening to the men there in the House of Commons. It is too great a work for us."

"Do you not have prospect of assistance?" asked the Archbishop.

"But," said Dorimène, "in case of trouble with the *caisse* we would lose all. And we have our future to think of and that of our children."

"When there is a law passed," explained Alphonse, "under which the *caisse* will come, that danger will be avoided. There will be limited liability. At the moment I solely am liable as promoter of the idea."

"It is dangerous that way." The Archbishop was emphatic. "You say it can be remedied?"

"Certainly. It remains to get the law."

"It is for a real need of our people, and who can doubt that? What is there to stop the law?" He fingered his ring and looked from one to the other.

For Alphonse and his dream a crucial moment had come.

"Your Grace," he said, "we have become dismayed in this work. We have thought seriously, as my wife has said, of giving up this whole business. We decided at last to seek your advice. Is it that this idea would have your approval or not?"

Archbishop Bégin began slowly: "The needs of our people are well known to us. They lack many things. This system of credit of which you speak is one of them. You have my thanks. You have the pledge of my assistance and my prayers. Be not discouraged. Work prudently. You have not only my approval, nay, more, I commend you; go forward in this work of justice and charity for the cause of the working masses. I will give you my blessing."

Alphonse knelt. Dorimène knelt, amazement lighting her face.

The hand was raised above them and they received the blessing of the Archbishop of Quebec.

Going home on the ferryboat, they remained silent. Alphonse's first reaction was one of elation. But he wanted to give Dorimène time to regain her composure. A load had been lifted from their shoulders. But when he thought a little more he began to realize that, in another way, a load had been fixed on his shoulders. The

Archbishop's approval was a responsibility in itself. Now he had to make good. There was no turning back. It dampened his spirits suddenly. He was like a man in a trance. Dorimène, noticing his preoccupation and busy with her own thoughts, kept her silence.

When they came in to their own house above the cliff and saw a small bundle of papers by the door of the little room that had been set aside for the affairs of the *caisse populaire*, it was too much.

She looked at the bundle as if it were a new baby.

They looked each other in the eyes. She came close. Both smiled.

"There is now, then, no longer any doubt, Alphonse."

Alphonse beamed. But the strained look had not left his face.

"We must go on," he said.

"We will go on." There was new firmness in Dorimène's voice now.

"All doubt is now behind," he said. "Just the same, it is a responsibility, this having Bégin's approval."

"Never mind. He will help to get the legislation put through."

"I am certain of it. He is very influential."

"That will take a load off."

"And there will be no great risk now."

"Alphonse," she said suddenly, "I will never again question this work."

"I know you were only trying to help me," he said. "But it was the cruelest blow of my life, just the same, when you doubted, Dorimène. It was the last straw."

"Forgive me," she pleaded. Her tears were falling now. "I tried to save you because I love you."

"And because I love you so, your doubting hurt beyond all. I didn't mind the criticism of the others who were calling me a crackpot. Not all of them! But you! That was terrible. It was the most terrible experience of my whole life."

She placed herself close to him. He took her in his arms.

"It's beyond explaining, all that."

"It's no longer important," she said softly. "There will be no more doubting on my part. The Archbishop has commended the work of my husband. From this day on, I am more than ever proud to be the wife of Alphonse Desjardins."

Alphonse could not speak. He was too overjoyed that Dorimène had withdrawn all her opposition.

He lit his pipe. Soon a curtain of smoke was in the room. He was a great smoker now. Dorimène thought that he must have about one hundred pipes; it was quite a business to know which one was "active," which one passive, just growing mellow, waiting its turn.

After a while he got up to go out. He must soon return to Ottawa. He wanted first to find someone to run the *caisse*.

"Wait," she cried. "You do not need to."

"But how?"

"Don't worry; I am going to run that *caisse*, and you will see that everything will go well."

It was unexpected, this depth of generosity. He knew that she disliked the work. He was reinspired. It was the riches of her giving that would now enable him to go on.

"It is on my knees that I could thank you," he said. "On my knees in the name of all those poor people who will one day have the benefit of this work."

Chapter 16

FROM then on things began to happen. The word got around that a group of people in Lévis had saved $40,000 in five years and had a little bank of their own. And people in other places started to do the same.

Alphonse tried to have legislation introduced into the House of Commons, Ottawa, that would permit and guide the development on a Dominion-wide basis. It failed. When it reached the Senate it was defeated by one vote. Defeat was upon the ground that such legislation belonged properly to the sphere of provincial lawmaking, not Dominion.

Alphonse drew up an act to be presented to the Quebec Legislature. He got the help of M. Ensèbe Belleau, a lawyer of Lévis. Sir Lomer Gouin was the premier of the province. Alphonse put this first draft in his pocket and went to see him. They were good friends.

"Here," said Alphonse in explaining the development so far of the *caisse populaire*, "is an opportunity for the legislative power to serve the interests of the working class."

The premier read over the act carefully, noted the objects therein detailed, and then said: "My dear Alphonse, you have prepared in that act for the economic independence of our people. I myself will sponsor it before the Legislature."

He did. It was passed unanimously in both Chambers. It became known in time as the Quebec Syndicates Act—and was considered a model in co-operative law. Alphonse was delighted. It put an end to the danger that had hung over him for years and which had been the source of Dorimène's fears. The *caisse* would become incorporated under the new law and he, as promoter, or any directors would have the protection of limited liability. If there should be losses, no one person would have to make good for them.

On September 27, 1906, *La Caisse Populaire de Lévis* held a special general meeting. Alphonse was in high enthusiasm. Seeing his good neighbors assembled before him, he was moved to express their intense joy and pride at what had been achieved so far. The members leaned forward to hear his speech.

It was an occasion to celebrate. The law had been passed. Best of all, it had passed without a dissident vote in either of the Chambers.

"The act is of the highest importance for our society and full of brilliant promise for the idea of which we have been the pioneers in Canada," he said. "We have now the protection of the law. The benefits which association can bring will be enlarged and multiplied and extended to other places."

His audience listened carefully. Some were spellbound. Some were dubious, having listened with large ears to the rumors of "crackpot," and a man "with a hobby of saving other people's money." But all were impressed. If Premier Gouin was passing a law on this thing, it must be all right.

"The Honorable M. Gouin has himself brought this law before the Chambers," Alphonse went on. "The working class is thus invited to partake of the great advantages of association in the economic field. He has faith in its wisdom and judgment.

"As for the future of the *caisse populaire*, all cause of timidity and hesitation have now disappeared." A faint clapping pattered through the audience.

"In fact our society can now get its growth, develop its operations, conduct its activities in the economic field, and extend to the workers of all kinds those benefits for which it has been founded, always guarding with jealous care its essential character of a purely co-operative enterprise.

"The vote of the Legislature is a ringing approval of the integrity of the view of the citizens of Lévis, the first to create by their hardy initiative the *caisse populaire*, thereby calling upon even the most humble workmen to band together in a new system for Canada!"

Loud cheers.

From that time the movement was really in motion. The laconic records showing the formation of new *caisses* had these entries:

1907
La Caisse Populaire de Paquetteville
La Caisse Populaire de St. Isadore
1908
La Caisse Populaire de Contrecoeur
La Caisse Populaire de Nomininque
La Caisse Populaire de Quebec, Faubourg St. Jean
La Caisse Populaire du Service Civil, Ottawa
And six others before the end of that same year.

Alphonse had now more than plenty to do. He was frequently called to meetings. He would be asked to speak, and afterward to spend hours instructing directors and committeemen. All his summers were taken up in this work. He asked no charge. In his journeys he got no expenses. He put his hand in his own pocket and paid. For lodging he stayed at the priest's house or at that of a friend.

Sometimes he took his lunch with him, having Dorimène put it up in a small bag.

Soon he was in great need of someone to help him.

One day he met the young Abbé Grondin on the Avenue Mont Marie. He gave him a great salutation and told of the victory in the Legislature. The work was pressing him. He needed assistance. There was need above all for a campaign in the press. It was the first Friday of the month.

"I have asked of the Sacred Heart of Jesus," Alphonse said, "that he find me a helper this very day."

"But you, yourself! You know most about that."

"I have not the time. My style is a little heavy. Why cannot you be the very man, Abbé Grondin?"

"But where would we publish our stuff?"

"I know Tardivel of *La Vérité* well. I am going to knock on that door. We will send our writing to that weekly."

Abbé Grondin said afterward that one fine morning, in the twinkling of an eye, he became a journalist. He started a stream of articles on thrift and credit. He soon included other aspects of co-operation.

Alphonse was full of plans for teaching the people. The busier he was the more prolific he became. He conceived the idea of the *caisse scolaire*. If the adults had not the habit of saving a little steadily, why not get it started in the children? He organized thrift clubs among the school children of Lévis. Their savings were to be put in the *caisse*. In a few months, $964 came in. This was mentioned in the annual report, and *L'Action Sociale* came out editorially and said:

The material result is considerable, the moral result is very much more. All boys and girls, learning today the value of saving cents, will become tomorrow a generation of thrifty persons. . . .

It is not strange that *L'Action Sociale* is particularly interested in this work. It is a kind that *L'Action Sociale* will specially favor and develop. It is a work that can effectively contribute to our economic awakening.

We give it today only our headlines. We wish especially to stir public opinion, but we will return on occasion to this subject, whether by ourselves or by the pen of a specialist.

Thus the idea spread. A number of people were asking, What is it this *caisse populaire?* How is it set up? What must one do? These questions came frequently. So Alphonse got the idea of a catechism of *caisses populaires*. Question and answer; that was what was needed.

He went at once to Abbé Grondin and asked him to write it. The Abbé demurred at first. But Alphonse persisted and Abbé Hallé gave helpful advice. Abbé Grondin started to write. Every night at the stroke of nine he would have a go at it. Under his little lamp, the questions and answers went down. Soon the presses of *La Vérité* were running off the first copies.

Publicity is a twin-edged sword. If it told the people what was to their advantage, it also told the enemies of the people's movement what was doing.

A rabid and unscrupulous opposition began to develop.

In all the feverish and fruitful labor of these years, Alphonse and Dorimène drew even closer and closer. She became not only his trusted aide in keeping the *caisse* while he was away, but also his counselor in the many points of policy that now came up. As the work progressed, as the societies grew and were able to help the poor, the two instigators could feel a sustaining satisfaction. He would pour over books, keep accounts, squint at columns of figures, write letters and more letters, make journeys and pay his own expenses—and all on $2,000 a year.

Their labors were dipped now in the splendor of a crusade and all things came out shining. It was for them a second romance. Their love had drawn the wider circle. They were going out after the least of Christ's brethren. Their family extended into all the parishes, even beyond the borders of Quebec—and before long, beyond that. . . .

Chapter 17

WITH a quick flick of his strong right arm, Paul Normandeau aimed his ax at the little chopping block that stood end up outside the logging camp.

The winter's work was over. *C'est fini.* The other lumberjacks were going, they said, "home." As for Paul he had to keep the word and all it meant out of his mind; he had no home. But he was going—where, he knew not.

Time after time he swallowed the lump that came up in his throat till the veins swelled and he felt parched. Even the little lumber camp had been a home of sorts. It was a warm, pleasant place to come home to after a day in the woods, sending across the little clearing its choice odors of frying pork or baked beans as evening messengers of comfort.

He straightened to his full six feet and his shoulders became square above his slender hips. He frowned savagely and with long fingers pushed back a mass of dark-brown hair. His eyes were pools of black brooding, his nose strong and slightly hooked, but what attracted most in his features was the wide mouth with a trace of the devil-may-care ever hovering at its corners.

Now that was over for another season. Yesterday the boss had driven in and paid off the chopping crew. His $240 for eight months in the bush snuggled in a strapped wallet in his hip pocket.

A pair of worn-out mocassins whizzed by Paul and landed in the remnants of a pile of firewood. Paul turned to see Leon Fournier, his crewmate during the past season. All day, every day through the winter, they had drawn the crosscut saw between them.

> Zing-zing, zee-zaw
> Clean and bright
> Quick as light
> Runs the saw!

They had sung their way, Paul and Leon and the crosscut saw, through the frosty, snow-clad valleys and slopes wherever there was timber to be felled.

"Little use lugging that sort of stuff home," Leon was saying. Then to Paul: "Say, bud, have you packed your bag?"

"My b-bag?" Paul stammered. "Oh, yes, yes! All the same, I haven't decided just where to go."

Leon looked at him slowly. He had never seen his chum so low. He began to feel sorry for him.

"Thought I might stay nearby somewhere, sharpen up my tools, and do a little woodcarving," Paul managed to say.

Leon knew well his skill with wood and chisel. He had seen him pluck an odd-shaped root from a swamp and with the skill in his hands fashion it into the figurine of a dancing girl. He could see the natural grace of wood and turn it into human form.

Now Leon's slow mind began to recall the story that Paul had told him one day out in the bush. Paul was an orphan. His parents had died when he was a baby, and he had been brought up in a sisters' orphanage in Montreal, where he had received a good education. Three years previous, at eighteen, he had had to fend for himself. His first job was on a river boat, but these were laid up in winter, so he had taken to the lumber camps and followed them ever since. With these reflections, Leon's good nature came to the surface.

"You'd be lonesome like a stray duck up here!" he said. "I'll tell you what. Come home with me. We have a farm and my father isn't too spry now. We might hire you at small wages in cropping and haying time."

Paul turned on his heel and his face brightened. It was good to be wanted somewhere. He went inside. The camp was in an uproar with men picking and sorting their sweaty clothing, their raveled mittens, and scuffed-out footwear. He turned up his bedding and packed his bag.

"Lead on," he roared at Leon when the latter came up. Paul flung out his supple arms in an excited and spacious gesture which indicated that his apprenticeship on the land was a matter over which there would be no debate at all.

The two companions walked out into the fickle May sunshine. Leon waddled. He was going home, fat and stolid, his simple soul as imperturbable as the grass roots. In the open air, he was always merry and whistling little tunes. Indoors, little was known of his mental state; as soon as he crossed a threshold to a warm corner, he immediately fell asleep.

Paul threw out long nervous legs in the sure-footed stride that had become habitual during his months in the woods. His gaze was constantly searching among the trees. He ran his eyes up the trunks of trees as if the artistry of nature fascinated him. The two wound their way downhill through slash and underbush; now and then when they came upon a sudden view of mountainside and lake and distant landscape, Paul must stop and watch the picture. Leon merely grunted and whistled another tune. He was hungry. At home the goose hung high. A change of cooking was a fine thing.

Ere nightfall they could see the village before them. It was a line of houses pasted against the lake shore, the narrow strips of land running uphill toward them. It was Lac Saint André. They reached the home of Leon's father. After a warm supper, they sat long amusing the family with tales of their winter's exploits in the woods.

The next day, when M. Fournier, a grizzled man and stooped of shoulder, beheld Paul splitting firewood in his dooryard, the question of his being hired solved itself. Paul was willing and

strong and neat. They would get at the fencing and cropping.
Then later would be the haymaking. On wet days Paul would be
on his own. This pleased him; for he looked forward to working
at his woodcarving every chance he got, and the Fournier homestead boasted a combination woodshed and workshop.

After their day's work in the fields, Leon and Paul went visiting. They sat on the cracker barrels in the village store, chin-
wagging with the shopping farmers. Paul soon became acquainted.
He went to Mass on Sunday to the village church where Abbé
LeForte, the gaunt priest, warned and shrived the penitent of his
flock. Every week there was a pie-social in the parish hall, and
they took that in.

Paul liked to walk up into the wooded hills that sloped gently
from the lake shore. One evening at the end of May, returning to
the edge of the village, he crossed the vacant farm of Henri
Chapais, who had pulled up stakes ten years before and moved to
New Hampshire. Now his farm was for sale to anyone who would
pay the back taxes. When Paul came around the corner of the
house someone was in the orchard.

It was Sandra MacKay, the daughter of the postmistress. He
had seen her giving out the mail from behind a low, rough counter in her mother's house, which stood just below the Chapais
farm, almost opposite the village store. Apple bloom was all
around in the little orchard, and she was evidently gathering a
bouquet. The limbs were too high for even her five and a half
feet and she was using a crooked stick to bring them into reach.

"May I help you?" he asked.

He leaped and brought lower a sprig of pink and white.

"Oh, such beauties!" She breathed appreciatively.

"But yes! I should rather say, the blossoms—they also are
beautiful."

"Well, *also!*" She laughed and there danced sidewise from her
blue eyes darts like sunlight on a rippling stream. Her hands attracted him. They fell firm and sudden out of low sleeves. But

what held him was the sure purposefulness of their every motion. When she slowly picked an apple blossom, it was as if she had already hugged it. Her fingers flicked and her hands went slowly about the branches like the sure sculptors of a soul's meditation. Poor, beautiful, frail little blossoms of God, they seemed to say.

Having perfected her bouquet of apple blossoms, Sandra turned to go in the direction of the village. Paul fell in step beside her. They faced the clear setting sun and walked down through the broad meadow carpeted with low, wild grass. Little clusters of maples, fresh in the green of their new leaves, stood guard at the edges, and robins sang in the branches.

Sandra's hair hung down in a great cluster of golden bronze. This golden bronze and the distant rays of the setting sun! Paul was dazzled. Her eyes, too, were blue—another testimonial of her Scottish ancestry, though she spoke only the French tongue.

Sandra was part of a phenomenon in Quebec; part of what some have termed the conquest in reverse.

At the battle of the Plains of Abraham in front of Quebec, General Wolfe, the invader, defeated General Montcalm. This was the conquest of New France by the British. Wolfe's soldiers remained to garrison the city, and in time some of them, it seems, married French women. It thus came about in two or three generations that families bearing Scottish or English or Irish names could not speak the English language.

Sandra MacKay had the bodily characteristics of a bonnie Scottish lass. But she had the manners, the expressive tongue, the sensitivity and élan of the French. In her person Sandra was the liquidation of racial animosities, a conquest in reverse, indeed. To Paul she seemed a major triumph of God and nature, and her presence filled him with a mixture of reverence and wild delight.

" 'Tis sad, is it not?" she said, "A vacant house like that."

Paul half turned to look at the old colonial house that was still in good repair, though weathered.

"It is old," he said, trying to speak calmly, "but well built with big strong timber."

"And the orchard!" she said. "I do love apples."

"The land looks good, too." Paul parted the grass with his heavy boots. "But one does not really know, as M. Fournier says, until one has put the plowshare into it."

"Oh, you, too, will be a farmer?" There was the slightest interrogation in her voice.

"Since I have been at the Fourniers, each day I am liking it better. And as for the woods, I have always liked that from the first day. It is my element."

"Perhaps you are descended from the *coureurs de bois*," she said impishly.

"It could be. They must have run very far. I have not seen them." His smile was a little bleak, and there was a run of compassion through her eyes.

"And you?" he said, "Mademoiselle *MacKay*?"

"Oh," she laughed, "on that side, some say there was a Viking who came to Scotland, then a MacKay to Quebec with Wolfe. And now here I am, Sandra MacKay." She pirouetted on the grass, holding up her bunch of apple blossoms.

Paul had never seen anyone so beautiful.

Quickly she became serious again.

"Our father is dead. My mother is a widow. I am the eldest of five."

Paul's steps slowed as they neared her house. He wanted to prolong the time to the utmost.

Paul told her his family history in brief and how he was alone in the world.

"And are you not lonesome here?" she asked.

"Yes, sometimes."

"Then you know where I am," she said graciously, with a flounce of her golden locks. "Besides it is the post office and you might be getting mail," she laughed.

Paul decided the next day he would be getting mail. He sub-scribed for the daily paper from Quebec. As a result M. Fournier began to become a great reader. He got caught up in the political articles and the great speeches of Sir Wilfrid Laurier and neg-lected to hoe his turnips and was actually glad when a wet day came. But for Paul it was an excuse for going to the post office every evening. Getting the paper was a certain protection from the too-observant eyes of the village.

But that was only for a time. Soon he thought no more of the village gossipers. He was too much in love to care what anyone said. They went together all summer.

On the morning of August fifteenth, the feast of the Assump-tion, Paul and Leon were up early. They were to go in a proces-sion to the church. Paul and Sandra, Leon and his betrothed, Cecile Briand, had planned to go to Quebec and join in the procession through the streets to Notre Dame de la Victoire, but they changed their plans at the last minute because Leon's mother had been taken ill. But they would take part in the parish gathering.

Nearly everyone turned out. They marched in line, whole families, friends, and neighbors. Paul liked these friendly demon-strations of country people. And how they prayed the Rosary! He had never heard the like of it. When they came near the church, they knelt; there was a statue of the Blessed Lady out-side. The Rosary started low and timorous. Voices joined all along the line, a little self-conscious at first but soon divested of all external awareness, this simple people plunged into the great drama of collective prayer. Faith mounted with each decade. The pleading voices of women—of mothers and grandmothers—led in the answers, telling in their tones something of the price which is paid for human life upon this earth.

Gradually even the indifferent found their voices and the vol-ume of answers rumbled and arose to Heaven in fervent petition, to her whom they knew as Mediatrix of Grace before the throne of the Most High.

Some had candles. Paul lit one for Sandra and she held it, kneeling on the roadside. It added something to the posture of supplication which, kneeling or standing, was hers. Queer how reverence magnified beauty, and religious faith made a person all the more exciting and mysterious.

All this he dimly sensed in flashes of distraction as they wer through the mysteries.

All that they were thankful for crept into their voices, the peo ple of the parish: all that they lacked, all that they wanted and couldn't have, all they had suffered, all that they yet highly hoped to be in the glory of a life to come, they told out in posture and voice and transfigured face.

Paul had never before felt so moved. In the woods, in the fields, and alone on the trails, he had felt the nearness of the Great Spirit. Praying together in the open air brought it to new point. The memory of this experience would go with him.

When it was finished they went for Mass. Abbé LeForte preached briefly on the Rosary. He explained how this prayer had been brought to earth and given to St. Benedict amid signs and wonders.

After it was all over the people met and greeted each other with much joy and talked. They were more friendly than at any other time—as if a new flow of life had been pumped into them. If people worshiped together, working together came that much easier.

Paul and Sandra went to the dances held every two weeks in the community hall. They danced sets, lancers and polkas. Every time Paul and Sandra, Leon and Cecile, lined up in the same figure. They met all the boys and girls and everybody was merry and full of fun.

"Join hands and forward all," the prompter sang out. It was a night in late September and cool enough for dancing. A wave of rhythm and commotion went through the line. The fiddler had drawn his bow; with it and his sensitive, sinuous fingers and the beat of his foot, he sent them flying and swaying around the floor. The strains of "Pretty Red Wing" and then "The Mocking Bird" rang out plaintive in the night, half-sad, half-heroic, but gay in movement and telling always the ageless story of lost love.

It all filled Paul with joy at living. But nothing compared to his happiness at holding Sandra in his arms.

Coffee and sandwiches and cakes were served at midnight just before the dance was over. They sat on the side and waited for the waiters, who came along with steaming pitchers and trays of food.

"Has Paul a cup?" asked Cecile.

Sandra laughed.

"No," she said. "Paul has no cup."

"Has he a saucer?"

Cecile laughed, too, this time.

"No, Paul has no saucer." It was Sandra again.

"And no bread?"

Even Leon laughed now.

Sandra repeated: "Paul has no cup, no saucer, no bread!"

She stopped abruptly, for there was a quick wound in Paul's eyes.

After all, he had nothing, he knew. He was not to inherit a ready-made home like Leon. Why must they be cruel in their jibes? Did she mean it? She could not.

But when she went to dance with Felix Gibier, he wondered. Was she becoming aloof? The evening was soon over and Paul saw her the short distance to her mother's house. They scarcely spoke. He bade her a formal good night. Sandra's mother, he knew, was strict with her and Sandra was an obedient girl.

The leaves were turning now and with the nights came early frost. The landscape paled; the northern lights grew bold and brilliant. Paul thought again each day of the woods and the lumber camps. Leon he knew would not return this year. He was planning to cut logs on his father's place and was looking for a partner.

As for himself, what he would do for the winter, and where he would go, he did not know. What did Sandra think? He must know. He had not been asked to her mother's house.

But there was the post office, and Paul asked her to go rowing on the lake.

They rowed out on the rippling waters in the twilight. Paul was proficient with the oars. He dipped and swung in rhythmic strokes and Sandra sat serenely enjoying the quiet motion.

"How different the houses look when seen from the lake!" she exclaimed.

Paul scanned the nearby shore. "Can you see Leon's house?" he asked.

Sandra craned her neck.

"There," she pointed. "Yes, there, that's their chimney."

Paul did not even look. But he said: "Leon is lucky. He inherits that."

Sandra was silent. She peered vacantly before her into the lake and sighed before she spoke:

"Yes, Paul, some are born lucky."

A sudden gust of wind came up and tossed the waters. Paul made mooring and hauled the boat in. It was almost dark and a chill rain began to fall. They walked toward Sandra's house.

"Will you be going this winter?" she asked.

"To the woods? Perhaps. In two weeks' time; even now, the camps are opening."

The rain came down and the wind tossed her hair.

"How I shall miss you, Paul." Her voice was full of longing and her eyes drawn with compassion.

The rain pelted down in torrents. They turned their collars. He took her hand and they started to run. But Paul must speak.

"Sandra, will it make any difference that—that I am not born lucky?"

"Paul, believe me, with me it would make no difference. But my mother," she gasped, "she says I must not marry, must not keep company with a man who does not have a house, or even a horse."

Her tears burst and mingled with the rain. Her sobs unnerved him. Before he could comfort her, she turned and fled into the house, leaving him enveloped in the rain, the dark, and the melancholy winds of autumn.

Chapter 18

OUT of it all Paul distilled an idea. The Chapais farm was for sale, he knew, and the house was habitable. It was said that this property could be bought for $700, the amount of unpaid taxes. Why, he'd borrow the money and buy it. The idea struck him as a great one. He'd put in $200 and borrow the rest.

Where would he borrow the money?

He heard of a moneylender who lived in the second parish away and went to see him. In the enthusiasm of his love for Sandra, his hopes were high.

M. Disco, the moneylender, who was also a lawyer, looked him up and down from behind a small desk, on which were a newspaper and a brief case.

"Do I have the honor?" he asked guardedly.

"My name is Paul Normandeau. I have been directed to you. I wish to borrow $500 to buy a farm in Lac Saint André."

"Hum! Lac Saint André," repeated M. Disco. "It is not a very progressive place. What property is it?"

M. Disco squinted one eye craftily. His eyes, when at rest, reminded Paul of those of the old owls, round and protruding, staring woodenly out of high branches upon all surrounding creation.

Paul told him, and he proceeded to foresee great risk in buying a farm which presumably another man, and a native, could not make successful.

"Normandeau?" he said. "I do not seem to recognize this name in the county."

"I came from Montreal," said Paul.

"Ah, your parents? Perhaps they are wealthy?"

"My parents! I haven't any. I am an orphan."

The round eyes resumed their owlishness.

"Then what security could you put up? You are not known in the neighborhood. No doubt you are inexperienced as a farmer."

Paul stared straight in front of him for a split second. He had come looking for a loan, not to be reminded of his shortcomings.

"You say you have worked in lumber camps," M. Disco continued. "Many lumberjacks are drifters, just drifters. Who could you get to go on a note? With no knowledge whatever of your character?" M. Disco shrugged. He picked up the newspaper that was on his little desk and began to read.

Paul thought immediately of his woods' foreman and Leon's father, and told him. But neither one was known to M. Disco. He turned him down flat.

"Young man, my time is very limited. Such a loan would not be wise for you, nor for me, I am sure." With that the moneylender picked up a worn brief case and quickly put on his hat and coat.

"But you see, I'm—I'm hoping to marry a girl, a nice girl, one from the same parish, and settle down there." Paul had blurted it out, half-desperate.

"It makes no difference," said the moneylender. "It's a little worse, if any. That's just the time when a fellow like you would plunge."

He hustled Paul out of his office and locked the door. "I am already late for court," he snapped and was gone.

Paul looked after the hurrying figure going to expound the

law. Blind rage rose within him. He felt his throat hot and dry
and his fingertips tingled.

It was dark when he reached Lac Saint André. The lamps were
all lit as he trudged heavily by on the road. It made him wince
to see what other men had—and many of them had it so easily.
Why must he be an exception? Around every one of those lamps
was a warm kitchen, food, the indefinable odors of home; there
were living rooms and bedrooms and cribs and cupboards. Here
love was made and life was made. Without this, life was lost.

Passing on the road, headed for his dull room in the attic of
the Fourniers, he lingered by a lighted house. The ache of the
homeless man was in him like a twisting fang. Outside in the dark
he drew close to the little gate that opened on a short walk,
lined with flowers and small shrubs. He stood silently to gaze
upon the cozy house and the stout barn which stood behind it.
He felt that hunger which a man feels with the all of him. It was
like looking upon something sacred and secret and forbidden.
Paul stood steathily, as the wild deer stands poised for flight and
peers at a human habitation. There was some strange fascination
in looking at what you couldn't have. It only made him the more
bitter to think of Sandra. He could never win her now.

The bridge to life was held by those who owned property—
a home in particular. Those to whom property was transmitted
by inheritance really did inherit life and the earth. The others
were wanderers as if in a desert. They were allowed to gaze upon
the sweets that others owned.

The thought made him bitter against his God.

The bridge to life was held, too, by the moneylenders, the
controllers of credit. Money was loaned for everything else. Did
they ever think of young men and women with the desire of life
burning in their veins?

The thought made him bitter against mankind.

Working at wages here and there was uncertain. Employment
was not sure. Sometimes a man was no further ahead at the end

of a year. On the other hand, on a farm there were several
things that could be made to pay. On the Chapais place there was
timber. Way back was an old stand of the finest. He had cruised
it. But now! He couldn't bear to think of it.

Saddened with his thoughts, Paul continued to walk the road.

It came to him that he should chuck it all. Yes, why not
leave the country and the woodlands that he loved and return
to Montreal? He would open a barroom and make suckers of
other men. If they were hard, one could be as hard. If they were
utterly indifferent to a man's need, he could be as indifferent as
they were.

But would he ever be able to forget Sandra?

Strange that it was now he remembered her the most clearly—
especially the way she stood and walked. He could see her now,
as he had so often seen her, standing behind the low counter in
the post office. It was the way she thus presented her body to
the world that was her charm. It was her gift at birth. It was some
touch that the spirit had made visible in her form, and no one
could even copy it. Sandra was the way she stood.

As if in answer to his question, there was a noise on the road.
A horse and buggy was approaching at a swift canter; amid the
clatter of hoofs, he heard the sound of indistinct voices.

He stepped to the side of the road where trees added their
shadows to the night and listened. Yes, it was Sandra's voice.
Soon the carriage drew by, the two occupants laughing and talking animatedly.

Paul recognized the man with Sandra. It was Felix Gibier, the
jewelry salesman who sold watches and clocks and rings throughout the countryside. He was a flashy person and sported a fine
trotting horse and a sporty new buggy. The horse slowed and
the carriage crept by. Paul stood watching as the wheels un-
wound contemplatively into the night. The back of the wagon
grew smaller and smaller to his gaze. Darkness poured slowly
in around the two heads. An impenetrable curtain had dropped

between Paul and life. He turned and walked slowly back to the village.

It was two evenings later when Paul came by the schoolhouse and saw that there was a light burning inside. He went to the door and could hear a voice. It sounded like someone addressing a meeting. He remembered that a meeting, the nature of which was vague to him, had been announced from the pulpit the preceding Sunday by Abbé LeForte. But something now in the voice of the speaker gripped his attention; he pushed into the back of the classroom and sank heavily into one of the rear seats. Just then the voice was saying:

"Where it is a question of workingmen needing credit, there now is nothing to hold them back. They can put their own savings together in the *caisse populaire*. From such a fund, loans are made to persons whose capacity and character are known in the parish. . . ."

Paul leaned toward the farmer who sat in the seat next his.

"Who is it?" he enquired.

"Desjardins," whispered the farmer. "Alphonse Desjardins, from Lévis, they say."

"The *caisse populaire* has been designed to complete the economic organization of the parish." The words came evenly and with easy conviction from the speaker who was standing at the head of the room by the teacher's desk. Paul saw a tall man whose shock of graying hair was thinning. There was a great healthy kindness in his large eyes and the heavy mustache did not hide the genial mouth.

"Whoever says there is not the need for such an organization does not know to what disadvantage a man may be put when he needs credit badly. If his friends and neighbors who know him have no system for extending a loan, then he must go to the moneylender and endure the cancer of usury."

Paul sat up straight on the edge of his seat. "The cancer of usury," he thought; "could it be any worse than going to a moneylender, anyhow?"

"Many of the young men leave the rural districts because, as your Abbé LeForte has said, there is no means to finance farming operations, not to mention the other group-owned services that are needed in a farming community."

Paul was electrified at the words. A new light crept into his dark eyes, as if from the reflected glow in those of the radiant stranger. He watched him, thrilled, and drank in every word.

God in Heaven! Someone did care for the plight of the homeless after all.

"It can be done by saving in regular small amounts. The law has been passed. That you should have a *caisse populaire* in Lac Saint André if you should so desire is now a law of the land. You must pick good directors for your organization and follow the rules. I will next tell you the success that has been made of those already started in Quebec. . . ."

When the speaker had finished, he said that if anyone wanted to ask questions, now was the time to do it. A farmer asked how much interest would be charged if someone wanted a loan. The speaker replied that this would be decided by the members themselves at their annual meeting. This annual meeting decided other questions, too, and laid down the main lines of policy for the whole year, he said.

Paul asked what a member had to do to get a loan. The main thing was character, the speaker said, that and the ability to work and to carry through the particular operation for which the loan would be made. Any man who was willing and able to produce should not be denied the use of credit.

Paul asked more questions. M. Fournier was there and looked kindly upon him. Other farmers, too, noticed his quick interest, and he became acquainted with a good half dozen during the discussion which lasted until late in the night.

The crusade of Alphonse Desjardins for a system of credit for the common people was under way. He knew his, and his knew him—when they heard him. Paul never wavered.

Chapter 19

Back of the opposition that developed to the ideas of Alphonse Desjardins were the monopolies and large financial interests. To them any wide movement for mutual aid among the common people was a threat. It was a thin edge of the wedge. Especially did it look dangerous when it was in the nature of a savings and loan system which led the people to develop their own finances.

To them this man Desjardins was like a Pied Piper going about arousing the common people to knowledge of the hidden power in their dimes and nickels.

He had to be fought. The weapons were various.

There was, for constant use, the sneer. Abbé Grondin was to call it "the grand enemy of all good works." The mocking smile! Who can stand before it? Youth, in particular, fall easily before it.

But there was also a job to be done in the field of legislation—obstruction.

It came about in this way.

In Quebec, the Syndicates Act gave legal status to the *caisse populaire* and other co-ops. There was no similar enabling legislation for Canada as a whole.

Alphonse now made a move at Ottawa to have an enabling bill brought in. He succeeded. As *Hansard* reporter he knew the ropes.

This bill was brought in as a government measure. It was discussed in the House. But then it was sent to a parliamentary committee for study.

This committee, in time, called for hearings. Those who wanted the bill must explain and defend their cause.

That is why such remarkable testimony came to be given.

For Alphonse, if he had developed enemies, had also developed friends. Of those in the field of religious leadership the reader has already learned. But what of the civil realm, which, after all, is where economic reforms have their place?

It would be hard to say what might have become of Alphonse and his movement at this point had not an unexpected ally suddenly appeared on the scene, as if from nowhere.

Chapter 20

THE man wore a cap and sport clothes. He was tall, bold, and had large eyes and a heavy mustache. He was mounted on horseback.

Behind him as he came along the street in Lévis one day in July were two more men, also mounted. And behind them were still others. But between the man who wore the cap and the further back entourage there appeared no visible communication.

In front of the *caisse populaire* the man stopped his horse. He gave the premises an appraising sweep of the eye and dismounted. He knocked.

Knock, knock, knock!

Someone was at the door again. It was like the same knock that had driven Dorimène almost out of her wits years before.

Raoul saw him first. Raoul was the eldest son, and was now learning to manage the *caisse*—a work to which he was destined to give his whole life. Then Alphonse came.

"Excuse me," said the stranger, "but have I the honor to greet Alphonse Desjardins?"

Alphonse smiled slightly.

"Er—yes."

"Then I have a favor to ask of you. I have heard, of course, of your work. The name's Grey, Albert Grey."

"Albert Grey?" Alphonse rubbed his eyes.

"I wish to make application to become a member of *La Caisse Populaire de Lévis*."

"Do you live near here?"

"Well, some of the time."

"And your occupation, may I enquire?"

"Governor General."

"But yes, of course, your Excellency!" stammered Alphonse. "It is a rare honor, I assure you."

Although he had seen Earl Grey in Ottawa, he hadn't recognized him now at first sight. The sport clothes deceived him.

Alphonse, for once, was flustered. The Governor General of Canada enquiring about the *caisse populaire*! The top of the nation politically! The top of the social register, too!

Alphonse swallowed with astonishment. Earl Grey, he knew, was not just another governor. He had stirred the imagination of all Canadians. That speech in Halifax on his arrival! Alphonse remembered the quotation from it that the press favored so much: "If you keep the character of your people high, virile, heroical . . . no one can venture to set the limit of influence of the Canadian nation."

Everybody had talked about it from coast to coast.

"I wanted to make sure I got here while we're staying at the citadel," Earl Grey was saying now as Alphonse showed him into the office of the *caisse populaire*.

"It is most kind of you to favor us with a visit," said Alphonse. Every year the Gover.er General and his lady spent weeks in Quebec City. They had a regular residence there, above the fort and the walled part of the city. Their coming, Alphonse knew, was always the beginning of a series of brilliant events in the social life of the aristocratic old city. Of these the levée, or reception, given in the official residence, was outstanding. The people loved it. Yes, *les Canadiens* loved it even. The strength with which they coveted an invitation to a reception at the Governor General's could only be matched by the vigilance and strength with which they opposed imperialism in every way, shape, and form in their press and sometimes on the political platform.

Alphonse opened the little desk in which he kept the books and records of the *caisse*.

"I am most anxious," said Earl Grey in French, "to learn of the principles upon which your bank is run and, if I may, look at some of the account books, the record of deposits, and loans."

"Your Excellency, it will be a pleasure," Alphonse said. How this Englishman could speak French! Yes, Alphonse now recalled that the English-speaking Canadians were being advised by this same man to learn French. An advocate of understanding he was, and he wanted to delve right into and see for himself the workings of the *caisse*. Well!

Then there was something to what the newspapers had reported, when upon his arrival they had described him as a social reformer—not to mention his having been private secretary to Queen Victoria, a sportsman, and world traveler.

"Take a chair. We will start on this one."

The two sat down together. Soon the records of the *caisse* were scattered open between them.

They talked and talked. Earl Grey asked questions. He knew about every phase of the need of credit among the people. He told Alphonse how the credit societies in Europe were working and brought news of other developments in the economic organization of the common people throughout the world. Alphonse was deeply interested and then delighted as he realized the significance of this new friend. They talked like men who found quick kinship in the spirit.

After a while Earl Grey said suddenly: "You are coming, of course, to my levée?"

"No, I am not." The eye of citizen Desjardins was straightforward and unflinching.

"But why?"

"My wife has received no invitation."

Earl Grey made a gesture of exasperation.

"Your wife has received no invitation?" he repeated. "I cannot understand such negligence! May I have the honor to meet Madame, your wife?"

Dorimène came in. Earl Grey bowed graciously.

"She is my best helper, my best counsel, in the work of the *caisses.*"

"I do not doubt it. I begin to see now the reasons for your remarkable success."

All three laughed.

The Governor General started to ask questions about the *caisse*, and for the next hour Alphonse explained thoroughly its workings. Then they examined the books and balance sheets.

It was near the time when the Governor General must leave. One of his attendants had entered with a message. He dismissed the man and said: "You know, of course, of the talk in the Parliament? A committee will look into your work and all that."

"They are holding hearings?"

"Yes, soon. Perhaps later in the month." A great trouble appeared in the eyes of Alphonse Desjardins.

"At least it will be an occasion to put on the records information about your work. And it will be of value for the people at large to know it."

Alphonse liked this man. He felt he could trust him. He felt he could trust him more than any man in Canadian public life, for he was above the quicksands of politics.

He said: "I am afraid. Quite apart from the committee, the interests that are opposing this will appear. They will make a fool of me. That will be their purpose. *To make a fool of me.*"

The man who had been secretary to the Queen and Governor of Rhodesia picked up his riding whip. He stood up suddenly as if a tide of restless energy spurted within him. Alphonse compared him to the type who had been adventurers upon the Spanish Main. The style of knighthood was in his gestures.

"They will make a fool of you, Alphonse?" There was a trace of surprise in the tone. "Then let me tell you they will also have to make a fool of me. And we will be fools together." He laughed.

"I—I do not understand." Alphonse was puzzled.

"I too will appear before the parliamentary committee and give testimony. Having now seen for myself how *La Caisse Populaire de Lévis* works, I can report on a most creditable development."

Alphonse was too dumfounded to speak. He had never dreamed of a man with the prestige of the Governor General coming to his assistance before a parliamentary committee.

"I am encouraged now," said Alphonse after a little, "more than I can tell you. Would it be possible for me to see you in Ottawa?"

"Certainly. There is need that we talk further. Just request an appointment through my secretary, and you will come to Rideau Hall."

Earl Grey next asked for a piece of paper. He wrote something down, passed the paper to Alphonse, shook hands, and left.

Alphonse and Dorimène looked at the piece of paper. It was a special invitation to the levée of the Governor General to be held at the official residence at Quebec.

Chapter 21

THE meeting was set for twelve o'clock noon. Earl Grey, the Governor General of the Dominion, was to appear before the parliamentary committee of enquiry. It was the talk of all who knew about it.

"The Governor General represents the King," remarked a member of the Press Gallery. "Must the King appear before the Commons?"

"He doesn't have to, but in this case he wants to. There is something in the wind there. Is it not very unusual?"

"Kingship was instituted in olden times," replied his neighbor, "to check the power of the barons. Today the world is run by money barons. Our critics are saying that the democratic parliaments are but the flabby servants of this plutocracy. I tell you, the king who is not afraid to throw his weight on the side of movements of the common people will find his prestige enhanced."

Down below, in the Commons, Alphonse sat at his desk. He was happy today. He was smiling—so much so in fact that he kept his head down for fear the others might accuse him of having a big joke up his sleeve.

He gritted his teeth and dove into his notebooks. Here was a "take" to be transcribed. But every time he thought of the talk that he had had with the Governor General in the latter's office he smiled again. Yesterday, Earl Grey had sent for him and they had been closeted for two hours.

"Alphonse," he had said, "sit down and let's talk a little more."

He had been so friendly Alphonse thought for a moment that he might be going to talk about cows. It was said that Grey knew personally all the good pedigreed cows in the county and how they were milking. But now he added quickly:

"It's about this hearing before the committee of the House. I wish to discuss with you just what points it would be advisable to set forth."

"I will be delighted," said Alphonse.

"You have been thinking over this matter?"

"Of course. I have thought much about it."

"Good. You know, Alphonse, if we are to be fools together we should look ahead a little."

They laughed. Alphonse felt relieved. Why not open up and let the Governor General carry the ball, so to speak?

"My idea is," he said, "the simple story. The simple story of what the *caisse* has done can stand on its own feet."

Grey nodded. "That—and added to that the story of what has been done in some European countries in the organization of people's credit. I am president of the International Co-operative Alliance and I have an advantage there."

What luck, Alphonse thought. There was no other man in the world at the moment as well qualified to go before the committee.

"Will you tell them of examining our *caisse* at Lévis?"

"I will. I will tell them I paid a visit in the early part of this month to Mr. Desjardins' bank. I will have no hesitation in saying that if a new act is required to facilitate the multiplication of banks like that which Mr. Desjardins, to his great credit, has established, the sooner that act is passed the better."

"And the books," cried Alphonse. "Tell them you went over the books." He was remembering the rumors that had been going around in Lévis. Big business concerns made a great impression by having their books audited by reputable auditors. An audit by the Governor General should rate well indeed.

"Yes," continued Earl Grey, "I will say that I examined care-

fully the books of the association and satisfied myself that the
bank was being conducted on safe business lines. I traced the
dealings with the bank of individuals whose names I selected at
random from its list of shareholders. I ascertained that the first
payment was ten cents, and then followed in several cases small
payments of about twenty-five cents at a time, until the sum of
five dollars stood to the credit of the subscriber, when he became
a qualified member or a shareholder in the bank to that amount."

"And had the right to vote at annual meetings," said Alphonse,
"as well as to apply for loans."

Earl Grey reached for his pad and pencil. "I've already notes
which I'll show you in a minute," he said. "Just want to jot down
some points as you talk."

"There is the record of repayment on small loans," said
Alphonse.

"Well, I saw it for myself in your records," went on Earl
Grey. "It's surprising. There must be a good moral tone in such
a community. I noticed myself that the members of the bank
borrowed small sums of twenty-five, twenty, and fifteen dollars,
and that these advances were repaid sometimes in small install-
ments, sometimes by single payment. The punctuality with which
small loans were repaid proved that the existence of this bank
has been of real use to its members in Lévis.

"Further, the usefulness of the bank was demonstrated by the
fact that over two hundred thousand dollars have been loaned
in small amounts since it was established six years ago. I was not
surprised to learn that this bank, like the co-operative and agri-
cultural banks in Germany, Austria, Hungary, Italy, France,
and India, notwithstanding the large number of its transactions,
has not lost a single cent."

"Too," Alphonse added, "wouldn't it be well to get in a good
word about the moral advantages, internally in the group?"

"Good. Go on."

"It supplies those persons who are known by their neighbors

to be good, thrifty, and honorable men with opportunities for helping each other and themselves in a manner conducive to the growth of those qualities of mutual trust and helpfulness which lie at the very root of good citizenship."

"Fine. Good citizenship. That is most important. And something that members of Parliament will appreciate."

"Ah, yes, the M.P.'s—but businessmen are not so easily impressed. They are more hard-boiled."

"Should I convey to the committee some idea of the moral security which your educational work brings into action in the *caisse populaire*?"

"Why, yes, of course," said Alphonse. "No one is allowed to borrow unless he is a member. No one can be a member unless he is voted unanimously by ballot to be worthy. Thus, only men and women who are known by the common consent of the people among whom they live to be worth-while persons can hope for admission."

Earl Grey made notes.

"There is then really a premium on thrift and character," he said.

"Yes, indeed. In addition there are rules to be followed in extending a loan. It is impossible for anyone to obtain a loan unless the management is satisfied that in view of all circumstances the loan is one which should be made."

"Are the purposes of the loaning limited?"

"Loans are limited to what are termed provident and productive purposes."

"I have that. Now look at my notes and make any corrections you will."

Suddenly Earl Grey stopped.

"But Alphonse," he said, "it occurs to me you may wish to present this testimony yourself exclusively. After all you took the risk of starting the thing in Canada, not me."

"Never mind that," cried Alphonse, his eyes blazing. "It's

better coming from the Governor General than from the *Hansard* clerk. Besides they are calling you first. You break the ice. Then I'll take my chances with the questions they'll ask."

Earl Grey's large eyes softened. "My dear Alphonse," he said emotionally, "you are most devoted to the ideal, this work. Your whole heart is in it."

"I am willing to stay in the background," replied Alphonse. "This work needs a strong ally, if it is to rise and grow and help chase away the demons that set upon my people in Quebec."

"You have, then, a deep religious motive behind your views and your course of action?"

"As I see it," Alphonse spoke slowly, "my people, and all people, are set upon by two demons. There is, first, the one that carries out the ancient sentence: 'Cursed is the earth in thy work . . . thorns and thistles shall it bring forth to thee,' as the Bible says. And in the sweat of our brow we fight for our bread. Then there is another demon. Call him Human Selfishness. Even when there is enough produced, even when there is plenty, he comes in and causes some men to seize all so that others have nothing. The union of these two demons is fulfilled in time. It brings forth the monstrous curse which is called poverty. By poverty vast numbers of human beings are damned before they are born, speaking of the body. Malnutrition, disease, ignorance, bad housing, distraught parents, bad environment, see to that. Against this I fight. I do not think it a great sacrifice that I stay in the background. No. I think that the greatest socially creative force is the spirit of sacrifice shown by Jesus Christ."

And so they went on for two hours while the Governor General lined up the presentation for the next day.

Alphonse had come away with a copy of these notes in his pocket. Now, seated at his desk the next day, he read with great satisfaction some of the words that Earl Grey was going to place in the public records.

Nobody who has any acquaintance with the life of the people can doubt that the establishment of a bank, formed on the basis of mutual knowledge and confidence for the mutual assistance of each other, must be of service not only to the members, but to the whole district in which they live. To those who are engaged in business come opportunities from time to time of making a cheap purchase if only the money with which to make the purchase is forthcoming, and the poorer they are, the more important it is that they should have the power of seizing profitable opportunities.

The farmer, for instance, while he is waiting for his crop to ripen, wants money in order to make a cheap purchase which will help the farm, or it may frequently happen to those members who are not farmers that the ability to make a cash payment in the middle of the month will enable them to secure an advantage which will benefit the whole family, but which they would not be able to make without a loan, in view of the fact that their salary is not paid until the end of the month. Here comes in M. Desjardins' bank. The member goes to the bank, explains the circumstances, obtains the loan, secures the advantage, and when he has sold his crop or received his salary he repays to the bank the loan he has borrowed from it. The bank has received in the interval a good interest, and the member has been able to secure the advantage of a good bargain.

A joint stock bank as a rule will not lend to an individual who has no security but his character to offer, but when a group of men known to be honest and thrifty and of good character, give their collective guarantee for the repayment of an advance, then experience has proved conclusively that a security is provided on which a bank can safely lend. The character of this security is shown by the fact that on the advances made to 2,169 Raiffeisen banks not one single cent has been lost.

God be praised! What a presentation this man Grey was making! He was making it this very day in the committee room not two hundred yards away. He was, Alphonse knew, putting it on the records in no uncertain way.

What luck! If I had searched the country from end to end, I couldn't find a better man to do this job!

As for his own testimony he did not fear it now at all. He would make it any time they called him. He would tell them the simple story. A pool of savings and credit among good neighbors!

Alphonse got busy and transcribed his "take." His heart was light.

Two weeks later Alphonse took the train for home. It was good to get out. Ottawa was getting hot as summer came on.

The House had closed; the hearings were over. Alphonse settled back in his seat and lifted the window shade, letting his eyes take in the sweep of receding level lands outside. A train was different and somehow restful. It was not like a Parliament where everyone was acting and overconscious of all eyes being upon him and estimating consequences. On a train you were your own little self. You were out of the swim and the current and could see things as they were.

How fortunate he had been in the past weeks. The hearings had turned to a complete vindication of his efforts. He would never forget the thrill he got when he read Earl Grey's testimony in the records. It had been given as they had prepared it across the table, only stronger. Grey had added his own observations of what the Danish people and also the working class of England had done through co-ops.

He himself had been called to the stand. Everything went smoothly, for the way had been prepared. His project had influential friends now. He told the simple story of the need of people's credit—and how it could be met. People could save. They could loan under rules and proper security. They could thus avoid the burden of usury. Could it work? Well, there was the record of the Caisse Populaire de Lévis.

That had been simple. Alphonse could only think upon it with satisfaction. Some other witnesses hadn't had it so easy. That morning session with Trowern on the stand, for example. He made a strong protest against the idea of co-operative self-help among the common people. It would, he said, cut in on the business of merchants and middlemen.

That very afternoon another dark horse entered the fray. Mackenzie King, Deputy Minister of Labor, was called to the stand. As Alphonse recalled that man's testimony, he smiled to himself. He stood up and took from the inside pocket of his topcoat a sheaf of papers. Among them was a copy of Mr. King's testimony. Worth having, that, when you went to meetings and wanted somebody to quote. Alphonse looked it over again, rereading a part he liked:

> . . . after listening to the evidence given this morning by Mr. Trowern . . . it seems to me perfectly natural to expect that anybody who is representing what is virtually a combine of retail merchants should be opposed to any movement that might have a tendency to check the possible effects of such a combine. Mr. Trowern's argument, it seems to me, reduced to its logical conclusion would prevent a woman from doing her own house-work.

Alphonse looked up from the page. In a minute he was peering past the other passengers in the coach.

How true it was! The right of the people to do their own work was constantly being taken from them by someone who wanted to do that same work at a profit. The people had their responsibilities skinned off them. In time they became non-entities. Yes, the mass man was a nonentity. He had been emptied. He had been cleaned out of his right to work and sweat and be responsible and plan and pray.

That's the reason he had so much energy for revolution. He was all pent-up and frustrated. His wrath could be terrible.

Mr. King had said other striking things. It was a movement most beneficial in educating the masses to help themselves. Credit societies could have a definite bearing on the cost of living and were needed especially among the working classes.

When the train reached Trois Rivières, Alphonse was still reading. He had on his side now not only the Governor General but the Deputy Minister of Labor. He was jubilant.

This summer he would put more vim than ever into the spread of his idea.

Chapter 22

It was late afternoon on a bright October day.

Paul Normandeau braced himself at the highest point he could get in the apple tree. It was a high tree, and from it he could see down into the farmyards all around the village. He could almost see into the chimneys of his neighbors, sending peaceful wisps of smoke straight up. There was something personal about a chimney. It was what made a house a human habitation. From his height, too, he could see far out on the shimmering waters of Lac Saint André.

Paul was not up here for scenery. He was picking apples. The tree was heavily laden with big red ones. Every one of its little branches was weighted down, bowing meekly with the clusters of fruit, some of which hung so close together that they crowded each other off as they grew and ripened.

My! thought Paul, what a wonder it is to see an apple tree from the *top down*, full laden and all ripe. Here one must stop and muse a little in the mellow sunshine and be caught in the spell of God's having provided—and provided with beauty. It was no time to think of sale and commerce and money-getting, and all the feverish rush and slavery that money-getting and money-spending dragged one into. It was time to stop and feel God about you in nature.

Most people, Paul reflected, see an apple tree from the ground. In harvesttime, or in blossomtime, this is a pretty sight. But it does not compare at all in wonder and mystery to a tree and its

ripened yield seen from on top. There a fountain of ruby joy
has spurted from the earth and then turned down. To Paul, this
particular tree, his best one, looked as if it had been sprayed with
life by a hand filled with incredible largess and power.

Paul, since first he had seen this tree, had never gotten it
out of his mind. Its blossoms he had pulled down for Sandra more
than two years before. Sandra herself he hadn't seen since that
night on the road. Shortly afterward her mother had sent her to
live with an aunt in Trois Rivières.

Paul looked down. Great God! What was there to compare
to owning your own land and the crops coming in?

How fortunate he had been to be able to buy the Chapais farm
through the *caisse populaire*. He had been able not only to make
repayments regularly on his loan but to save a little besides. His
experience had taught him the value of thrift, and the *caisse* was
making that thrift fruitful before his eyes. He aimed to save
one tenth of everything that he earned and put it in the *caisse*.

He attended all the meetings. Once when it came his turn to
speak, he said that everyone should save one tenth of what he
made and put it in the *caisse*. If everyone did that, they would
soon have a fund of credit in the parish, enough to do anything
they wanted. That very first winter he had cut enough logs to
pay more than half the price of the farm. He had worked a
partnership with Leon Fournier, who had married Cecile. Paul
had been able to have his meals at Leon's house. He worked
all his spare time on his own property, repairing the house and
the barns and bringing the fields back to cultivation.

He filled his basket with apples and came down. He went up
again and down and up. He filled boxes and barrels.

Great God! Yes, now he spoke it as a prayer. There was
nothing like owning your own land.

When you worked for wages you could only have increase
during the hours that you were working.

But here, with land, God worked increase for you all the time

—even while you slept. You did the chores and God was busy all
the time growing grass and timber, and wheat and oats and
apples. It was a great life as long as a man didn't splurge too deep
or get nervous at the failure of a crop now and then.

He felt thankful for the goodness of the harvest. No wonder
the best songs were written in Thanksgiving at harvesttime.

Was he becoming too pious? He bit into an apple. It tasted
so luscious that he was struck with the goodness of God's
providence all over again.

He stopped picking. He sat down on the grass under the tree.

What little kingship a man could have on this earth was here:
to see the land alive, to feel in your palms the solid orbs of the
apples, to look down a yielding acre of good ground and realize
that ten thousand stems stood up to feed you—the thought of all
this nourished you in at the heart and extracted all the bitternesses
that you might gather from having suffered at the hands of your
fellow men.

The land was life—and life bearer. To own and till it was
divine. Yes, the land was holy.

That evening when they sat to supper—Paul and Leon and
Cecile—they talked of the Parish Fair that would open on the
morrow. Prizes were to be given for the best products. There
would be livestock and vegetables and fruit, while the interior
of the hall would be decorated with samples of homecraft, mostly
by the women, but also by the men, for craftsmanship has never
been allowed to perish in Quebec. Afterward there was to be a
supper in the hall, announcement of the prizes, then a meeting
of the *caisse populaire*, and then a dance.

"Will you put in your exhibit, Paul, or not?" Cecile asked this
question and gave an arch glance at Leon.

There was no answer.

"Woodcarving," said Leon, "is very scarce. And it is such a
piece!" He laughed and shook his head from side to side, and
with an air of great conviction went on: "Never have I seen

anything like that except once a long time ago in an art shop in Quebec."

Paul smiled. It was pleasant to hear the enthusiasm of his friends over the little statue he had carved the preceding winter, using the stormy nights when it was not fit to be out. It stood about eighteen inches in height and was carved from a carefully selected piece of ash. It wasn't so much the height as the width with which he had had to start in order to get the effects he wanted. Out of the solid ash he had carved the figure of Sandra MacKay standing behind the low counter in the village post office giving out the mail.

"These fairs," he said, "they should be limited to good cooking." He reached for another slice of cold lamb. There were fried potatoes, fresh made chow from their garden, fresh milk, and pumpkin pie. "No wonder Leon is getting so fat."

Paul was bronzed, his hands calloused, his face thin.

"Just the same," he went on, "I will go to the supper and to the meeting of the *caisse populaire*. As for the craft exhibit, what if the original herself should be there?"

"And what a thrill if she would see that!" said Cecile.

"No," said Paul. "No. She might not like it."

"But why?"

"It does not do her justice."

"It does, I tell you. It looks just like her."

But Paul was obdurate.

When he had gone out, Cecile ran upstairs and returned.

"Leon, it is still there."

"What?"

"The statue in his closet."

"Yes?"

"Leon, why can't we take it and enter it in the exhibit under Paul's name?" Cecile was breathless.

"Sound scheme," said Leon. He was shaking with laughter. "Bring it down. I'll hitch the horse at once and we'll run right

over with it. Can you imagine him when he sees it set up in the
Hall tomorrow night?"

"And Sandra?" Cecile put a finger to her lips and pondered,
"Her mother's expecting her any day, I've heard."

Leon rushed out to the barn mumbling to himself in glee:
"My wife is a genius." ·

On the day of the Fair the parish was full of activity. Many
of the products of the countryside were on display. Visitors
came from outside and agronomists were present from the Department of Agriculture in Quebec.

Outside on the grounds were pens full of chickens and turkeys
and lambs and calves and even colts. There were tables of fruits
and vegetables. Inside the Hall, the main table which ran the
full length of the building was reserved for the supper. On
smaller tables around the walls were craft exhibits.

When Paul arrived it was already late in the evening. The place
was full of people, some thronging the Hall, others seated at
tables and partaking of the sumptuous fare.

Abbé LeForte was presiding and was already half-through
announcing the decision of the judges. Paul had seated himself
at the table and given his order when he heard the Abbé declare:

"We now come to the winners in craftsmanship. The first
award goes to a piece of woodcarving. The winning artist is
Paul Normandeau."

Paul raised his head in astonishment and wished he could fall
through the floor.

"Hold it up. Hold it up for the people to see," called Abbé
LeForte to the boy who stood by the table of exhibits.

The boy seized the statue, held it up in both hands, and as a
ripple of hand clapping went through the Hall and shouting
began he moved it slowly from left to right as if in the performance of a strange rite that had suddenly excited the minds
of the crowd.

Everyone recognized the statue on sight. It could only be

Sandra who stood like that. A perfect tumult of laughter, wink-
ing, nudging, and talk went through the Hall. Hearing the commotion inside, the people who were outside crammed in through
the doors.

Out of the corner of his eye, Paul caught sight of Leon and
Cecile coming in. They were trying to look innocent, he could
see. But behind them stood another figure. It was Sandra.

Abbé LeForte was still trying to get attention. With the
instinct of a true teacher, he seized the moment.

"We must congratulate our new settler in this parish," he said.
"He is a valued member of our *caisse populaire*. He has not only
found land here, but he has found beauty. And best of all, he is
able to transfer it to wood."

Loud laughter. "Cheers for the woodcarver! *vivre, le graveur
sur bois!*" went through the room.

The boy swayed proudly with the exhibit. Sandra stared as
though her eyes would pop out. Then blushed and hid her head
modestly.

"Unless we can create beauty in our own environment, we
cannot have a culture, we cannot have contentment in the villages. In the making of things in our own homes there is first of
all use. But there is also beauty, and if beauty makes contentment
and self-respect it may, in the long run, have more use than
anything else." Abbé LeForte was enjoying his speech more than
a sermon.

"Best of all it is the practice of the arts in the home that teaches
men and women to work under their own inspiration. The artist
is lavish with his labor. He has to be; otherwise he does not
create. There are persons who are too mean to start any creative
work, wondering first what they will get out of it. They thus are
hoarders of their skills and mind power and, nine times out of
ten, never develop but must go about looking for a master who
will hire them. When many fall into this state, there are not
enough masters to hire them all, and they swarm from city to

city looking for masters, and there is great fear and strife. The land becomes vacant. Art is the will and power of self-employment. When the teaching of art declines, civilization is soon stricken with a convulsion.

"Now," he said, "let's go on to the winner of the second prize."

While he was fumbling for the name there was a dead silence in the Hall.

It was then that Sandra, all defiant of onlookers, red hair flying, crossed the Hall. She sat down beside Paul.

"Paul, I've come back."

He smiled at her.

"There's a dance after, Sandra."

"Paul, will you save me all your dances?"

"Of course. But Sandra—there's a meeting first. Desjardins is to speak."

"Desjardins? Paul, I too must hear this man."

At eight o'clock the meeting was called in an upstairs room of the Hall. The treasurer was half-through his report when Alphonse Desjardins arrived. He heard the report which told of their shares and deposits and the amount and condition of their loans. The board of directors, the supervisory and credit committees, also reported. He checked their books and their bank deposits, which were kept in the nearest branch bank. He complimented them on what they had done in two years. They had settled a vacant farm and extended numerous other smaller loans. That was good. Thrift as thrift was good; thrift turned to creative loans was better.

Desjardins was no mob orator. He did not trust mass emotion nor resort to crowd-pleasing clichés, knowing that out of these stunts came the demagogic types. Rather he was the meticulous builder. He wanted to find persons of integrity, to inspire and instruct them carefully in step-by-step building of the credit society as he knew it at the time. He hoped the work would spread outward from them. He knew that ultimately persons must be trained for this work.

Now to the members of the Caisse Populaire of Lac Saint André he repeated his most persistent message:

"The purpose of the *caisse* is to complete the organization of unity within the parish. This unity has been incomplete up to now because there did not exist any organism to supply the credit needs of the people. The *caisse* is designed to fill this gap and create a reservoir of money and credit, to be placed at the service of all the worthy members.

"It is important to organize the rural people, and the first indispensable organism that should be given to them is the one which will contribute directly to the accumulation of capital of which they have need to revitalize their industry and make fruitful their power, permitting them to escape the poverty-making yoke of capitalism represented by a swarm of people who live from their labors without bringing anything themselves to the national wealth.

"Here it is necessary not to let ourselves be intimidated by those pretended sages who counsel an exaggerated prudence when, at bottom, they are only the echo of their own intellectual deformity, or victims of a deplorable professional grouping who have accustomed themselves to fear all innovations. Their minds, all enveloped in fog, cannot have any conception other than that of routine or of *laissez faire*. They call that prudence.

"There is such a thing as a fetish for things as they are, good or bad, and a ridiculous timidity. It is necessary to be wise, without doubt, but also to have a measure of boldness with reason. It is not necessary to imitate the poor ignorant ones, full of defiance toward those who speak for them with loyalty and disinterestedness, but having confidence in the first fake who wishes to see how things are going along before joining a new movement that the highest social authorities have recommended.

"Our people like a sensible and prudent progress and they do not fail, by the grace of God, before the reasonable responsibilities which impose themselves. They do not fall for the bait of wood lice or timorous moles; they leave the fearful ones behind and set out cheerfully to follow those who have social authority, who come to them with wisdom and without false promises, but also with courage and sincerity in action, showing them the practical way to get out of the rut and triumph over the obstacles.

"They understand the truth of the old saying that people learn by doing, and the way for the people who want to run their own affairs, without the burdensome tutelage of anyone, is to band together and take the advantages as well as the responsibilities which result from joint control and of access to the full economic life. This is the indispensable corollary of the civil and political liberty that we enjoy.

"Without economic independence the electoral ballot is in large part a mirage."

When he had thoroughly explained the purpose and end and functioning, he set about to incite their hopes of the future.

"If such saving as this is carried on regularly for some years by the members, consider what funds shall have been accumulated. As you organize your thrift now you get experience in giving small loans on approved projects. Later you will have large funds. It can all be built from your own thrift. Then you can go into large projects. Then the people can have co-operatively in their own parish a store, a bakery, a hatchery, an abbatoir, or any other service within reason that they need."

Thus did he sow over Quebec the seed of economic reform in the villages.

After the meeting was over there was a big dance. Some of the older men jumped on the floor to try to show up the younger fellows.

Why should anybody be sad when there was such a good spirit in a community? The dance lasted until near daylight.

The next day everyone was saying that Paul and Sandra were engaged. They were married before Advent and went to live on the once-abandoned place of M. Chapais.

Chapter 23

THERE were thousands of others like Paul. There were thousands and then tens of thousands who were helped by joining a *caisse* and getting loans, the vast majority of which were for lesser undertakings than buying a farm.

They borrowed when they were hard-pressed, for a provident or productive purpose: to shingle the roof, to put in a furnace, to have a baby, to buy an overcoat, to bear the cost of their father's funeral, to buy seed to put in a crop, to dig a well, to buy a pure-bred bull, to equip a fishing boat. They borrowed, in fact, for every imaginable need under the sun.

There were many, indeed, who were helped toward thrift and livelihood by these small credit societies.

Now the idea had friends, not only in the high circle of religious leaders, but in the civil realm as well. As for Alphonse, he was a man driven by other men's needs and by his own creations.

Six months of the year in Ottawa, six months in Lévis! Most of the latter time he spent promoting the idea. Year by year people in all walks of life became interested. He received many letters. This correspondence grew large and voluminous. All these he answered in his own hand. He had no stenographer and no carbon copies were kept.

The number of societies increased. Nearly all soon multiplied their funds. Constant demands were made upon Alphonse.

There was recognition from abroad—Pierre Jay, bank commissioner for Massachusetts, and Edward A. Filene of the famous

Filene store of Boston were asking him to come to the United States. They wanted to see how a credit union could be organized and they wanted also a law drawn up. He went. On the same trip he founded the first credit union in the United States. This was in Manchester, New Hampshire. Soon others were started.

The Russell Sage Foundation asked him to New York to tell of his work in building a credit system for the people. The same credit union law that he had prepared for Massachusetts was in time adopted for New York.

The same year President Taft invited him to Washington. This time it was to a conference of state governors and also to the Southern Commercial Congress. He was invited to join a group which was going on a study tour of Europe. This, he felt, he must decline because of the obligation of his work in Quebec.

The State did not honor him. He remained nothing more than a *Hansard* reporter all his days.

The Church did not pass him by. It was announced that Alphonse Desjardins was to be made a Commander of the Order of St. Gregory, in recognition of his services to the working class. His work to extend the social doctrines of Christianity to the everyday life of his people was not to go unnoticed.

Alphonse was a worker. He only made $2,000 a year. He was a worker trying to do something to help the workers. He had a home to keep up. He had traveling and out-of-pocket expenses educating people how to use their own credit and build on into the future.

When, therefore, he heard that certain details relating to the ceremony of investiture with this honor would cost him a small sum of money, his old stubbornness flared up.

"No," said Alphonse, "this is not well."

"But it is an honor," admonished Dorimène. They were sitting in his little office.

"Even so," said Alphonse. "You know what my costs are this year in traveling here and there! Carrying my lunch in a little paper bag!"

"To be decorated like that by the Pope! It is very rare."

"Had I not been able to put up at the priests' houses very often these years, look at how much more it would have cost us to carry on our work."

"I do not know of one other," said Dorimène.

"One other? What?"

"Who has been thought worthy of such an honor."

"That does not change my point," said Alphonse. He crossed to the desk where the books of the *caisse* were kept, returning with the manuscript of an article he was writing for the *Bankers' Magazine*.

"A Commander of the Order of Saint Gregory!" breathed Dorimène with awe and admiration in her tones.

"Dorimène, I feel not. Not when it will take that much."

"Oh, but Alphonse!" It was pleading and disappointment now.

"No. Rather it should be a trip for you, Dorimène. Working always here in this house and never a change. Yes, a little trip for a few weeks."

Someone rapped at the door and was admitted to the office by one of the family. It was Abbé Grondin. He had come to talk with Alphonse over the writing he was doing for the *caisse populaire* movement.

"What do you think of this man?" cried Dorimène. "He is offered a decoration by the Pope and instead offers me a trip to the country. It is not equal!"

Abbé Grondin sat down, his bright face lighting up with humor.

"With all respect to the Pope," said Alphonse, "I have not asked for this, and I don't feel like paying the costs involved. If I am worthy, let those who think so give the decoration to me."

"Well," said Abbé Grondin, "considering what you have to spend out of your own pocket to travel for the *caisse populaire*, I don't blame you! But in all good causes a way is found."

Dorimène's face brightened, but she remained silent. Abbé Grondin went on: "You know, since I became a journalist, I hear

the newspaper gossip. There is talk of Alphonse Desjardins' being
made a senator."

For a moment all were silent.

Alphonse half-turned to his desk and poked a batch of letters
into a pigeonhole.

"Talk," he said. "Just talk! Paper stuff!"

"Just the same a sign of right thinking," defended Abbé
Grondin.

Alphonse smiled. He loved the priest with the good face. He
leaned back in his chair for a moment and stroked his mustache.

A *Hansard* reporter in the Senate! He could do great things for
the *caisse* there. To be a senator you had to know so many things
and oversee what others were doing. But was that for him?

Aloud he said: "Even if it were so and I could qualify, what
could I do in the Senate to stir up wage earners and farmers to
organize their own credit system and manage their own money?"

"With all respect to the Senate, this job in the villages is fundamental," said Abbé Grondin.

Dorimène crossed the room and picked up a volume of *Hansard*.

"Read it," she said, "from cover to cover, the record of the
Parliament. How seldom does it come near to the secrets of economy as a poor man must face them day by day!"

"That, my dear, is our mission," said Alphonse. "You have
named it: the secrets of economy as we know them in our kitchen.
The Parliaments oversee and make policies. They take their cues
from the economist—one who has studied premises in the abstract,
from the standpoint of investors, of industry en masse, or a social
class—theory in bulk with an eye on the going concern as is. But
we shape our action from the experience of the average man
going out to win bread for his family. We turn up spots on which
heavy dust has lain. I will stay at this work."

"Which is to say that much of what passes as education is
false." It was Abbé Grondin holding up a startled finger. "You
are too polite to say it, but I will say it. In the big universities

they study a great thickness of ponderous tomes. And the graphs! Like the ski runs on Mont Tremblant, I tell you, curving all around the slopes. But they chart the course of impersonal economic forces. The problem is not being attacked from the personal and human viewpoint."

Dorimène closed *Hansard* and the book banged upon the table. her words came quickly: "Who was it that said, 'the economy of a nation begins in its cottages'?"

"We live," replied Alphonse, "in a time when too much has been taken out of the cottage. For years there has been going on a concentration of capital, a concentration dangerous by its effects, against which it is necessary by consequence to take action. Capital is drained out of the parishes, to accumulate in the great centers from which agriculture can draw no benefit. This destroys the equilibrium necessary to prosperity in the country. The combines do not operate for the benefit of the consumers, nor of the little producer, nor of the farmer. For example, the farmers of our province who wish to buy a farm machine have to deal with two trusts. This is no longer a natural situation. At the end of each season the price is fixed before it is known what it should be. In Canada, forty-two men control almost two-thirds of the wealth."

"This makes life dull in the villages," said Abbé Grondin. "People follow the exodus of capital. They go where employment is." Alphonse nodded.

"Of course. The sending away of savings into the large centers favors this concentration and this abuse. It sterilizes indirectly the whole countryside.

"Our neighboring Americans say that one millionaire costs a hundred thousand poor people. And we ourselves have been making millionaires for the last twenty-five or thirty years. One of the great causes of depopulation of the country is an abnormal development of industry in the large cities by reason of the influx of capital from the rural parishes. The farmers are thus deprived of the means to improve their soil and replace their machine equipment, their means of production.

"Without doubt it is better to place money in the bank than in the bureau drawer. But it is still better to put it to work in the parishes than to have it go and make fortunes for speculators and brokers.

"The remedy is to husband and restore the money of the countryside and create there a reservoir in which it can be held. And these reservoirs are the *caisses populaires*. Some fear not being able to use the funds thus accumulated. It is an error. It is easy to employ capital. And it is astonishing how it serves to revive initiative and to improve farming methods. Besides, agriculture is a practical industry. It has need of capital to make it prosperous. Colonization is also an activity which augments the riches of the country. However, who furnishes to the colonist the necessary capital to overcome his obstacles? What organization is able to aid small industry in the villages? That is the work of the *caisse populaire*."

Alphonse stopped and wiped his mouth with the back of his hand. He pulled his chair closer to Abbé Grondin. Dorimène went over and began to pick up the letters which lay open on the desk.

"I talk too much," said Alphonse. "One would think I was giving a speech. A fine way to treat a visitor in my house."

The two men laughed.

"Not at all, Alphonse. I need it. Helps me in my articles. You have analyzed the causes of the decline of the village economy and culture—in a word the lack of social organization in the villages."

Dorimène listened as the men talked on, her ear cocked.

Alphonse attracted his kind, she knew. There was the young man, Cyrille Vaillancourt, who drank in her husband's ideas. What a pity he was not here now, she thought!

Fundamentally, it was not merely a system of credit that Alphonse was seeking. It was that and more. Dorimène remembered that Abbé Grondin had written to Alphonse to get a list of books and literature which would help him in writing his catechism of the *caisse*. The recommendations which Alphonse had given showed clearly that a much wider co-operative organization of the community was envisioned. It included stores and whole-sales, producer co-ops, bakeries, fire and life insurance. Alphonse had searched in the Library of Parliament at Ottawa for text-books. Those he could find at that time he recommended. They were mostly about co-operation in Belgium.

"If you kill the productive spirit in the outlying regions," Dorimène could hear her husband saying, "the know-how soon dies, too. To decentralize there must be not only the productive arts but also local credit. In the long run there must be some de-centralization of finance. Co-operation should be tied in with decentralism. . . ."

On his desk was a copy of a well-known magazine. She turned the pages and saw an article on the work of Alphonse Desjardins by Louis Brandeis. It was an example, it said, of what could be done to offset the dangers of an uninterrupted concentration of economic power.

There was a letter, too, from the American Bankers Association. The secretary wrote to say that Alphonse had been a great in-spiration to many among them. Would he favor them with an article on his little banks?

Notwithstanding these comments from abroad, Alphonse went his modest way. He had his work and his home. Their sons and daughters, seven in all, were a happiness: Raoul, Ann-Marie, Edgar, Adrienne, Albertine, Paul, and Charles. Adrienne was to be a nun. Paul would take up dentistry. They were blessed in that their children were well able to look after themselves.

Alphonse would go on with his work, she knew. Always meet-ings and more meetings. He must leave home and travel. He must leave Dorimène at home in charge of the household and *caisse*.

Very often his travel expenses would come out of his own pocket.

Dorimène saw the prominent names on the roster of *La Caisse Populaire de Lévis,* among them Archbishop Bégin of Quebec and the Honorable C. A. Pelletier, Lieutenant Governor of the province.

How near she had been to a failure in opposing all this in the frail beginning!

And now the proffered honor from Rome! Dorimène felt fiercely proud of her husband. And suddenly she had an idea. She remembered his anxiety about unity and good order in the movement—an anxiety that grew as the number of new banks increased throughout Quebec. Certainly there must be someone of prestige at the head.

She waved her hand for attention: "Leader of the *caisse populaire,* and Commander of the Order of St. Gregory! What prestige! That should silence the critics and the enemies!"

"An honor richly merited," said Abbé Grondin. "Besides, most timely and useful!"

Alphonse felt his defenses crumble in one blow.

"Just the same," he said, "if an honor is to be given there should not be required an outlay of money. That is not a good way."

But Dorimène had won her point. With her competence and foresight, she could manage; she could take care of all. And he received the honor. He became a Commander of the Order of St. Gregory.

Chapter 24

M. DISCO, when he came out of the main door of the Montreal Windsor Hotel, looked straight across the street. The *calèches* were standing in their usual line, the horses flicking their tails lazily in the September sun.

M. Disco picked his way carefully across the busy street, his owllike eyes rolling nervously from side to side. He hailed one of the drivers and got in. Soon they were jogging downhill in the direction of St. James Street.

Anything but merry were M. Disco's thoughts. He leaned forward tensely, one hand above the other on the cane which he held between his legs. Something must be done to stop this devilish business of the *caisse populaire*. It was getting too hard to loan money now; borrowers were getting too independent. Surely a financier like Dykers would be able to do something. He had connections in political circles and knew publishers of newspapers. Yes, Samuel Q. Dykers was the man! Like as not his old friend Dykers was not aware of the way these Desjardins Banks, as they were coming to be called, were spreading.

An hour later the two were still in close conversation in Dykers' office.

"The future is very black," M. Disco was saying. "I myself have had to move twice already. The *caisse populaire* comes to the area, and soon no one comes to me to borrow. A few more years of this and we won't be able to loan money except at very meager rates of interest." The tones were confidential, the countenance melancholy.

Dykers listened quietly. He was a stout, almost jovial-faced man, dressed in dark gray. Outside business he was humanitarian; in business hours his eyes had a troubled coldness in them and the mouth was hard. Money he looked upon as a machine to be used for the multiplication of itself.

"To what extent are these *caisses* now competing in the small-loans field?"

Dykers' question was cool and even. It was still only three thirty in the afternoon, and he was not one to get excited over the anxiety of even an old friend.

"Do you know that the oldest one—the one at Lévis—has loaned over two million dollars and never lost a cent? Never lost a cent yet, and boasts about it!"

Dykers only permitted himself a slight elevation of the eyebrows.

"What did these people have to start with?" he asked.

"My dear man, you may not believe me but their first deposit was only ten cents. And not so many years ago."

"Indeed?"

"And you can realize," went on M. Disco, "how serious the situation is when I tell you that the same *caisse* now has $549,000 in deposits."

"Is there any proof that other places can follow the example of Lévis?" asked Dykers.

"I'm afraid so," said M. Disco. "This Lévis thing is being copied as a model all over the province, in Ontario, and in the States."

"But not every place has a man like this fellow Desjardins to head it up."

M. Disco looked encouraged for the moment. "Just the same," he went on, "there is no place where I can feel secure to conduct a loan business at the old rates of interest."

"Consider too," added Dykers, "that these *caisses populaires* may go crashing to the wall in a few years. Then good old times will return."

Dykers exuded confidence. He leaned over the desk and eyed M. Disco craftily.

"Of course," he said, "there are things that you and I can do to help along their going to the wall."

"Like what?" asked M. Disco.

"Well, in the field of public opinion. Spread around the idea they are not safe."

M. Disco's eyes stuck out.

"You know," continued Dykers in the most decided tone, "the moneylender cannot arouse sympathy or public opinion in favor of himself. He has been an unthanked character right down the ages, so perverse is human nature. But we can arouse opinion in favor of the banks. The banks are in good order, generally. *Leave banking to the banks.* That is the idea we must put in the minds of the people."

M. Disco looked in admiration at his old friend. But Dykers did not return either the glance or the admiration. Instead his glance trailed out the window over the rooftops. Maybe the small-loan shark *was* doomed before a movement like the *caisse populaire.* But he, a big financier, could find ways. Meantime, Disco's struggle for survival could be made a little useful.

"What did you have in mind?" asked M. Disco.

"Alphonse Desjardins is to address a meeting in a small town near here tomorrow evening. Why don't you go out and ask some of these questions before the audience?"

M. Disco looked pleased but perturbed.

"But I am not a public speaker."

"You don't have to orate. Just ask the questions. You may depend upon the suspicious capacity of the human mind to do the rest."

They talked another half hour before M. Disco agreed.

Alphonse was thinner now. The strain of appearing before an audience brought a temporary flush to his cheeks; on his face was a haggard look; at times he carried himself with difficulty.

But when he spoke it was with the same old effect—a blend of dignity and friendliness.

He had many examples now that he told. Some were of how people had been helped by the *caisse* through the years. Some were tips on how the business system of the *caisse* was to be run. And, for good measure, he told some of the points he had made when he appeared before the Committee of Parliament: that education was the essence of co-operation and that in the field of credit the blight of usury had to be checked.

"There were in Lévis," he said, "two or three loan sharks before the foundation of the *caisse*, but God only knows where they are today."

It was at this point that M. Disco felt the most uncomfortable. For the moment he wished he hadn't come. When Alphonse had finished he rose to ask his questions.

"Mr. Chairman, why should people talk of starting a *caisse populaire* when there are banks to serve the community? Why not leave banking to the banks?"

The chairman bowed toward Alphonse, and he replied:

"That is a good question. Yes, there are banks. But is it right to expect of banks a service which their purpose and method do not especially encourage? The commercial banks, however, serve a necessary and important function.

"But in the case of the *caisse*—and there are people here interested, because I have had correspondence from them—we are extending credit to a new field, to persons united by a moral bond of association. Actually, we are supplementing banking.

"Give the banks their due. That is not to say we must concede to them monopoly rights upon the use of our own money.

"The role of the *caisse populaire* is social. And it is of the parish. The ordinary banks are inspired by a different thought. The aim of the *caisse populaire* is moral and educational; the aim of the bank, with all respect, is stability and its earnings. These ends, so different, must answer your objection."

Alphonse was used to answering such questions and welcomed them. The years of study and correspondence with authorities in Europe stood him well. He could turn the questions into telling educational effect on the audience.

M. Disco returned to the attack, awkwardly.

"You mention the amounts that are being saved in the *caisses*. What's going to happen to all this money? In the future what will happen? And who will look after all this money?"

"As the movement grows," replied Alphonse, "the existing *caisses* will be federated into a central for guidance and safe conduct.

"This step is already being studied. There is no need to be timorous and enter into despair. People learn by doing. And with the good spirit a way is found to overcome all obstacles."

M. Disco could get nowhere. He was glad to remain as quiet as possible for the remainder of the meeting.

Alphonse could conclude from such experiences that what men lacked most in our time was a social conscience. They had lost that. To many, and otherwise good men, no such thing existed.

So he wrote a little pamphlet in which he said:

All civilized peoples have recourse to organization, putting together their energies. Shall we because of apathy stay behind and leave to others the direction of powerful social forces? No, assuredly not. Let us go on with activities of high purpose, knowing that our people can count on the warm solicitude of our true leaders.

The harvest is ripe to the sun of social love, its promises are rich, its premises are high, and the harvesters cannot help but go forward to their beneficent work.

If there is one everlasting duty that the world imposes, it is the social duty. Its conception has been obscured a little by the notions born of the revolutionaries, but Leo XIII has brought it back to its place of honor that it should always have occupied. That duty commands our participation.

Go to the people, they will listen to you. Aiding them in their daily struggle, one will bring them to love the more their Faith and their Fatherland.

Chapter 25

DORIMÈNE was glad when Alphonse was superannuated. He now no longer would be away in Ottawa.

His health was failing again. She knew.

He was staying more and more in the house at Lévis. Dorimène had set up again as nurse and comforter. And it was not like the illness that he fought off in the strength of youth. He was not young now.

As for Alphonse he would take the body for granted as long as it would last. When he learned that there was little that could be done for him, it was mainly of his work he thought.

Then, too, he began to worry about how hard Dorimène had worked. He reflected that if it hadn't been for his dream of the *caisse populaire* she would have had more leisure and a better time in the world.

On the evening of January 25, 1920, the nineteenth annual meeting of *La Caisse Populaire de Lévis* was held. The founder and president could not be there. Everybody was sad.

But Abbé Grondin was there. By this time he had become intimate with Alphonse in their long working together for the movement.

This was sometimes now called the mother *caisse*. It had a fine record. The members had saved regularly and the total of them all made a very large fund. They had made a great volume of loans to their members over the years, without a loss. They were a model. Their success had inspired all the others.

When Abbé Grondin got up to speak everything was hushed, for they felt he was going to say something of their founder.

"I regret," he said, "not to see among us the figure of our founder, M. le Commandeur Alphonse Desjardins. A serious illness confines him to his house. I ask all the members, especially the children whom he loves in particular, to pray that he may be restored to health as soon as possible. His work is not finished. We need him for a long time yet to guide us by his counsel and experience.

"If it were not that I am sorry for his illness, I would be happy at his absence. It permits me to go back to the past and to say things that I couldn't say if he were here. It permits me to sum up the sacrifices he made for twenty years to assure the success of this work.

"Sacrifice! To him it was necessary to make known to the world this work of universal and social value which has already served the people of our little city. He sacrificed his leisure, and all his leisure. If he had so wished he could have rested from the long months of fatigue accumulated during the federal sessions of Parliament.

"He did not do that, because he understood that the citizen has not fulfilled all his duty when he has provided for himself and his own, but that he also has a duty toward society as a whole."

Abbé Grondin paused to drive home the point. The members of the first credit union in North America sat silent, hushed and attentive before him. He was older now than when he had sat *sous une petite lampe fumante* to prepare the first arrows of propaganda to fall on the land. The sensitive face, though more mature, was still humorous and had the quick gift of receiving and transmitting good impulses—as if it were a chosen reflector of the all-teaching spirit.

"Alas," he cried, "how few understand this duty!"

It was in effect the same message that Alphonse had written for his followers: "If there is one everlasting duty . . . it is the social duty." If the world veers from it, it must at last come back to it, in rags and sorrow, in strife and hate and bloodshed. *"The harvest is ripe to the sun of social love . . ."*

The great thoughts that the *Hansard* reporter had so well expressed warmed them all. They had seen its effects. Abbé Grondin said:

"Alphonse Desjardins sacrificed not only his leisure but also his money. You would have to see the books, as I have, to realize what was the cost of the numerous trips in this work. These sacrifices he had hidden from everybody, even his close associates, and had it not been for a slip on his part we still would not know the sums of money he has spent to assure the success of his work."

And in this vein he went on. They sat in the cold January night and began to remember the good deeds their founder had done.

It was his custom, they learned, when he went out on trips to found new societies, to ask for his out-of-pocket expenses. Sometimes a friend would put him up for the night and give him his meals. Thus he would save fifty cents here and a dollar there. In such cases he used the little funds saved to defray in part the costs of printing pamphlets and circulars needed in the work.

Alphonse sat at his desk in the little room of his house set aside for the affairs of the *caisse populaire*. It was late at night, but he had been unable to sleep. Instead he pulled together some of his notes and began wearily to push his pen across sheets of paper.

He had heard of the fine things that Abbé Grondin had said of him at the meeting. They cheered him. But just the same he was worried. What if cheats and fakers crept in? They might exploit the idea for a time for their own. Then the whole movement would be discredited and it would be years before it could recover.

Many groups of people had started little credit banks. A goodly number were successful. There was frequent absolute proof of their great value. But it took someone qualified to look after their affairs. It took intelligent and interested directors, and they were not always easy to locate. Obviously someone must find and train such persons.

That is what he had been doing these years since the movement had spread out from Lévis.

After he himself was gone, who would do it? Who would there be to transmit the experience of one *caisse* to another, so as to avoid mistakes and have good bookkeeping and unified practice and things running smoothly?

More clearly than ever he saw now that there must be a federation. His illness delayed his action on it, but with so much time for thought he became the more convinced of its need. So he would draw up a letter and send it to the different *caisses* and get the leaders thinking about what they must do.

Dorimène came in to find him bent on his task.

"Why do you spend yourself at this when you should be resting?" she asked.

He stopped writing and looked up at her.

"Dorimène, there are one hundred and two *caisses populaires* in the Province of Quebec. There are thirty-one thousand persons banded together for credit. They have built assets of six million three hundred thousand dollars. And that is only one side of it."

"It is the great work you have done."

"Each one was formed independent of the others and still remains so."

"You are not satisfied with that?"

"No, Dorimène. They should be joined together. Then what one learns the others may benefit by, and many other reasons."

"Ah, yes, it is the federation of which you are thinking again."

"It has always been my dream that these societies should be united in federation. They have done it that way in Europe."

"But, my dear, why not wait until you are recovered? You should not be exerting yourself now."

"Even so, Dorimène, my work would not be finished if this idea was not launched and well understood. I must go on."

And he went on to draw up the letter to his followers in the locals.

He said in it that in spite of his health he felt the time had come to consult them regarding federation. He asked their advice. He proposed federation. He also proposed the formation of a central *caisse populaire*.

Addressing "My dear collaborators," he said, in part:

"Someone will say, perhaps, that the provincial government could bear the costs of this federation and thus avoid the expenses that could fall on the *caisses*. That I will oppose with all my strength for it would be to place our *caisses* under the tutelage of political parties and under a patronage always detestable and which would cause the death of this good movement."

This was the gist of the letter which he wrote laboriously and sent out. It was his last letter.

To the end he mistrusted party politics. In party sponsorship of social institutions, he saw only an outcropping of a patronage system "always detestable." Such could be advantageous for a time, but it could not be a permanent way.

As the months passed, his strength waned. He was confined more and more to his house and room. Now in thought was he borne back upon the past. Though he was sick, his mind was free to wander among the deeds of his lifetime.

He became thoughtful. For days Dorimène could not arouse him out of it. She besought him, saying that if something was worrying him, he should tell her. He remained silent.

But at last he must speak. He called her and said: "Dorimène, open the drawer of my desk. Get the little notebook that you will find there."

She went to the little desk and pulled out the drawer. She was tired. Her body lurched with fatigue. Her eyes were ringed and watery and her face was drawn; the weariness of a life's crusade was upon her.

"Here it is, Alphonse."

He did not take it or even look at it.

"Look at the end," he said, "at the bottom of one of the last pages."

She turned the pages of his notebook and found the place.

"That figure there, added up, is the total of my own money that I have spent in organizing the *caisses populaires*."

"Oh, yes."

"Do you see it?"

"Yes."

"What is it?" The total was $4,119.43.

"Yes, that money, it should really be yours, Dorimène, and here I have taken it away for the *caisses*. Before I die, I ask you if you are willing to give it to me."

"But Alphonse, that money, it is yours; it was you who earned it. You have the right to dispose of it as you wish."

"That is true. But that money I have earned, we have earned together, for the one and for the other. If, instead of using it to promote the *caisses*, I had given it to you, you could have used it, for example, to travel a little. You could have taken a change and a rest, you could have had a maid more often, and today you would be, perhaps, less fatigued."

Dorimène watched his thin face while he spoke. There was almost a sob in his voice, and as for herself she couldn't speak. When he ceased she turned her eyes past his to the window and into the distance.

"No, Alphonse."

She looked through the window as one seeing far off. She was thinking of the young man, of whom he had told her, who had been able to buy a farm and settle down because a *caisse populaire* had been opened in his parish. She thought of the many others who had been able to get loans when they were in need, scores of thousands taught thrift, and a pool of credit set up within their reach.

"No, no," she repeated in loving and gentle tones. "I would not have it otherwise."

On a chill morning in autumn, Alphonse awoke from a dream. With his eyes still shut, with all exterior contact of the senses cut off, he remembered vividly the strange scenes through which his subconscious mind had just carried him.

He had been a small boy again playing on the streets of Lévis. It was an evening of winter and his mother called him in. She sent him for a loaf of bread for their supper, giving him the last five cents she could find in her purse.

It was already dark. It was cold. The frost traced weird figures upon the windowpanes and great shapes hung high in the gloom between the lampposts. He ran to the store.

He asked for a loaf of bread and offered his coin. But the clerk scowled and said harshly that it was not enough. Alphonse said it was all they had, but the clerk became angry and shouted:

"Go on, now. Get out of here."

Alphonse began to shiver with fear. He looked up at the counter and saw a row of loaves, doughnuts, rolls, and pies. He started to cry.

Just then an elderly man came into the store. He took a small basket, put in bread and pies, and said kindly, "Now run to your mother." He was the owner.

Alphonse dried his tears. He smiled. But going out the door he cringed because he saw scorn and disdain in the eyes of the clerk and he knew the look was pursuing him. Into the dark that harsh scowl followed him. On his way home he ran and ran but he felt it hovering in the shadows of every dark corner and magnified to the proportions of a monster—a giant with a cruel mouth and great boots halfway up his body, trampling all small things before him.

In the deep, vast, fast-fleeting reverie of his dream, there came other scenes.

He had dreamt again and again, recrossing the stored imagery of his whole life. And lurking in the background of them all was the same scowling, skulking monster. Only in shape did he change; always in essence was he the same: Selfish Indifference, that giant of iniquity, the sum total of the world's sins of not-loving. In shape now this was no longer the giant of childhood but a spirit of evil.

He it was behind the critics who had almost persuaded Dorimène to give up just after the beginning. He it was behind his own fears when a Committee of Parliament was about to investigate and a quick and potent ally had stepped out of the unknown.

He it was behind the deadly lethargy of the poor whom he had tried to arouse; and when they were aroused, behind the dissensions that budded and grew among them. Always implacable foes he and Alphonse Desjardins had been. They had stalked each other through a lifetime.

The strokes of a bell, at first far-off and faint and ethereal, then closer and positive and earthy, came through his senses from the outer world. It was the bell of Notre Dame de Lévis just across the street ringing for Mass. He stirred and opened his eyes and shook his head. It was a relief to be free from the fears and conflicts of his dream.

It was well, he thought, now fully awake, that he had spent their money as he had. Dorimène wanted it. He would die in peace.

It was better, come the close of one's life, to have done something to try to kill the monster that grew so easily among men. He was glad.

He called in those who were necessary to make a disposition of his affairs.

He wrote in a private note to a nun:

"I have made four times the novena to Mother Marie of the Nativity to obtain my wish. But as I know that it is not possible to force the will of God, I ask you if you in your community would kindly join with me in a fifth novena to beg your sister to obtain for me that which she believes to be the most useful according to my condition; I ask also that she take under her protection the work of the *caisse populaire* so that she will inspire in those who will take my place the spirit with which they are to be animated; and that she will bring about a federation to consolidate this work which does an immense good."

Dorimène took the letter from his trembling hands. She read it. It was her man's last plea for the institutions he had created.

It was sacred. She placed it in an envelope and sealed it. She herself would take it to be mailed.

It was October. She put on her coat and fixed her hat. Her hair was all white now. Her face had still a vivid beauty, but there was a meekness in it and the eyes were compassionate—all together that rarest touch of the divine artist upon the human countenance.

Dorimène walked slowly on the street. A neighbor stopped to enquire: "He has been anointed?"

"Oh, yes."

"Ah, but there is nothing to fear, Madame Desjardins."

She lifted the lip of the little mailbox and poked the letter in. Her hands dropped empty by her side. It was gone, Alphonse's message. He had sent out a call for help to those who prayed. He was canvassing the saints to give a hand in the work. She turned thoughtfully away and began slowly to retrace her steps.

Fifteen years! Fifteen years had passed since that day she and Alphonse had stood before Archbishop Bégin. On that day she had given up her own will, the will of the natural woman to make a better place in the world for her children. And in its stead she had put the cause of the least brethren.

Well, she had nothing to regret. All had come out well. The family was prospering. Raoul was working with *La Caisse Populaire de Lévis*. Edgar was a doctor.

As she walked in the morning sun, Dorimène enjoyed the freshness of the air. The change from the sickroom had cheered her for the moment.

But suddenly October veiled the sun and a host of dark clouds rode in from the north. Dorimène felt chilled.

October of the falling leaves!

Its spell was clutching at her heart. . . . October of the night frost, painting great splotches of color through the tree tops . . . October bleaching the landscape, as the leaves withered and fell and trees took on their widowhood . . . and the little muted voices in the grass were lulled to sleep and the gray sky fell close and looked more somber day by day.

She quickened her pace. She was glad to close her own door behind her, going at once to his room.

"Dorimène," he said weakly, when she came in, "come here."

She put her head down so she could hear him whisper.

"Without you there would never have been any great movement of the *caisse populaire* in Quebec. You must know that. And bear it in mind."

She turned her head and sobbed noiselessly till her hair tumbled about her face. But he was too spent to notice.

It was the aloofness now and the austere finality of the figure in bed that hurt her most.

By late evening his breathing became more difficult. He asked to be assisted into a rest chair. He sat straight up for a time. Toward midnight his head was bowed . . . and they saw him falling forward.

On November first a Quebec newspaper came out and said: "M. le Commandeur Desjardins, founder of the People's Banks in North America, is dead. One calls him without fear the benefactor of his race."

For two nights, lights burned in the house at the corner of Guenette and Blanchet streets. People came and went slowly in little groups, and spoke in lowered voices. His numerous relatives, men from the *caisses populaires*, and persons distinguished in public life were among them.

For Dorimène they were two days of receiving, two days of condolences:

"So very sorry, Madame. We were all shocked."

"Such a loss! A place is left that is not easily filled."

"I wouldn't believe it unless I read it in the papers."

"The public is very stirred."

The townspeople, too, came to kneel by the silent coffin and its untroubled tenant, aloof in that awful dignity. They lowered their heads and their words were blurted and came tumbling. Some wiped a cheek and whispered among themselves.

"What a man! He stuck to his idea twenty years ago when we were all pouring the cold water."

"His movement is bringing aid to the people in every part of the Province of Quebec." "Did I ever think I would be saying this at the wake of Alphonse Desjardins? But it is we who were the fools." "His place is not going to be easily filled, I tell you."

And so they talked and talked, neighbors and friends and relatives, deep into the small hours, speaking with a frankness that death alone can bring.

The morning of the funeral dawned with the imperiousness of an event that cannot be canceled.

Abbé Grondin had finished the Rosary. Dorimène glanced over her shoulder to see the house filled with men and women rising from their knees. She rose to her feet, but was immensely buoyed by the tender human compassion all around her.

Notre Dame de Lévis, just across the way, had been made ready for the funeral.

The bier was already in the front of the church when Dorimène entered. The pews were filled with people. Dorimène walked ahead of the mourners to the front, the whiteness of her face like a diadem above her black.

As she stopped to kneel before the altar, she felt a tremor of surprise at the people she saw.

That figure kneeling in the sanctuary was Archbishop Bégin—now Cardinal of Canada. He was there praying for Alphonse. There, too, were Monsignor Roy and the Canons LeFlamme and Beaulieu.

In the front pews knelt His Excellency the Lieutenant Governor, Sir Charles Fitzpatrick; the Hon. Alexandre Taschereau, Prime Minister of the Province of Quebec; the Hon. Adelard Turgeon, President of the Legislative Council; Sir F. X. Lemieux, Chief Justice of the Superior Court; the Hon. Judge L. N. Belleau, the mayor of Lévis; Mr. J. K. Laflamme and the aldermen; the members for the County of Lévis, Dr. Alfred Roy and Mr. Boutin Bourassa; and Ernest Lapointe, federal member for Quebec East.

The divine service was celebrated by Monsignor Gosselin, assisted by Abbés G. Desjardins and Rodrigue as deacon and subdeacon.

There, were, besides, a group of priests from the College of Lévis, clergy from far and near, and delegates from various *caisses populaires*.

The church was filling up. Dorimène could feel the pressure of the crowd pressing into the back pews. A man, a poor man, whom already the newspapers were calling the benefactor of his race, was not to be forgotten.

The sorrow of it swept over her and she sobbed bitterly when the choir began to sing the Kyrie Eleison. This part of the Mass poured out with her all the sorrow and desolation of the bereft human heart, all pleading for forgiveness, all supplication for comfort and understanding on the lonely journey. Here was the ultimate in grief. Here the heart was to be emptied.

But not for long. In a few minutes the Requiem had progressed to the Dies Irae. That which you kneel before is your God, a living God, no symbol. In a moment grief is to be struck down with majesty. In the measured tones of the Dies Irae are stirring notes of triumph, speaking ever to the vanquished heart and snatching it from despair and telling in the thousand wordless ways of music that the maker of life is also master of grief and death.

Dorimène felt the burden of her sorrow being shifted. She was not alone carrying it at such a moment.

Death was a social happening, too. How strange it was! Only thus, in the religious climax of death's high hour, the greatness of life's plan was thrust suddenly through the gloom! By this faith, a man could go on serenely to his end, come what may.

It was too much. It was more than she ever expected. In some way death's sting was being drawn.

When the Mass was over a great throng followed in the chill November morning to the cemetery of Mont Marie.

Dorimène bent and wept by the grave, knowing now the final cleavage. She heard the rough clods fall and the fresh, damp thumping of the clay, as Mother Earth packed her primeval insulations around her own. It was over. A circuit of human life was closed.

What would the future bring to the name of Alphonse Desjardins, to him who had dreamed to help his fellow man?

Below, the St. Lawrence, fixed and one in the wide movement of its waters, flowed seaward to the tides of God as it had flowed for ten thousand years.

Epilogue

It was one day in March, 28 years later. I was standing by a small statue of Alphonse Desjardins at the headquarters of La Federation des Caisses Populaire at Lévis. Rosario Trembly, assistant manager, was saying:

"Out of the foundations of Alphonse Desjardins, there has grown 1,080 caisses. All together they now have over $200,000,000 in assets.

"In short-term loans they extended a truly vast amount in aggregate over the years. The losses have been almost nil. They have extended $60,000,000 in long-term loans.

"There are now ten regional unions or centrals," he said. "Each one has its clearing house, as cheques are used."

"And the Federation," I asked, "what is its function?"

"The Federation is the central for these unions. It carries on the function of education and inspection."

This wide development, I learned, had come about during the directorship of Cyrille Vaillancourt, who had been Alphonse's young follower. In addition to his managerial responsibilities, Cyrille Vaillancourt kept alive the spirit of the founder through the publication *Revue Desjardins*. Some call him today the "second founder."

Dorimène, too, I learned, had been of much assistance in the years following her husband's death (she survived him by twelve years). She gave her counsel in line with what Alphonse had planned.

Their house at Lévis had been given over to the *caisse populaire* federation by Miss Albertine Desjardins, their youngest daughter.

In the United States. I already knew about the development in the United States. The societies which Alphonse had initiated took the name of credit unions. With this inspiration and also with ideas gathered from Europe and India, the wealthy Boston merchant, Edward A. Filene, gave generous support to education and promotion. Credit unions began to spread throughout the United States. Under the leadership of such men as Roy Bergengren and Thomas Doig, numerous societies were formed and federations, or leagues, as they are called, set up in every state of the Union.

Today, there are over 9,000 credit unions in the United States. They have accumulated savings in the neighborhood of one billion dollars. Their loan service extended to the needy since their inception runs into a total so vast as to be almost unintelligible.

In Nova Scotia. In the early 1930's the Extension Department of St. Francis Xavier University included credit unions in its program of adult education for social action. Since then societies have been established in the Maritimes and have spread to all the English-speaking provinces of Canada.

Nor does the movement stop here. Far beyond these frontiers does it roll. From this point of inspiration, social students have taken the pattern to many parts of the world. Credit unions are being formed in the Caribbean, in South America, in Newfoundland, and in more places than is possible to mention. There is every indication that it will continue to grow as more people realize the power that there is in thrift and in the management of their own funded money in their community. This limit is not easily set.

It was not until the end of June that I was able to return to Lévis. I went to see Abbé Grondin. He was in his room at the College of Lévis. He stood up when I spoke of Alphonse Desjardins and his work. There was with us another priest of the

College, a man so modest he would not have his name mentioned. "I am sitting on his chair," he said.

It was an old swivel chair, and there was a faded reddish cushion. We talked about those early days. After a little while, Joseph Trumel, an inspector for the *caisses*, who happened to be in the building, came in.

After the usual introductions, Joseph Trumel said: "A trunk has just been discovered which contains some of the letters, papers, and correspondence of Alphonse Desjardins. It is at my house, a few minutes' walk from here."

We sat down to a tasty luncheon and talked. But we were really anxious to see what the old trunk contained, and shortly we were walking across to the house.

M. Trumel carried out the little trunk and placed it on the floor. He turned up the cover. We saw packets of letters and files and envelopes. They were mostly requests to Alphonse Desjardins for information or replies to letters that he had sent.

From one of the packets there fell away two sheets of note-paper of the ordinary small tablet size. We picked them up. They had been folded once. We opened them and spread them out and began to read. The small, clear handwriting was in the French language. We read:

A prayer for the work of the caisse populaire and other similar works:

Sacred Heart of Jesus, I beg of You the special grace of Your divine light.

If I am making a mistake, enlighten me, and inspire in me a strong aversion, a great dislike for the idea that I would pursue and which is the aim of my work.

May I repel it with a sort of scorn, if it is Your good pleasure and make it disappear from my mind. If I should never think about it again from this moment I would be a thousand times happy.

Remove from my heart all false vanity, all impractical desire, all chimeras and foolish dreams.

If You wish that I persevere in this way, oh my God, fill my weakness with your strength; clear away the obstacles or give me the means to surmount them.

In this case as in the other give me the most perfect resignation to your holy will.

May your purpose be mine, may your desires be as commands to me.

Deign, oh Jesus, to direct, to inspire my activities toward whatsoever be the end of your eternal purposes; bring it about that I may find perfect harmony with your will in the hearts of those who follow me, but especially in the heart of my wife, the beloved companion of my life.

That she should always be my consolation and my help, whether you inspire me to the complete abandonment of these projects or to the thought of accomplishing them. Amen.

It was Abbé Grondin who spoke first:

"That prayer! It is most important! A real document of guidance, I tell you. And the reason? If any movement rises in the name of the masses and is not God-centered, it quickly gives into the hands of a few men too much power. The power-seekers gather round. And this breed, let me tell you, is worse than the money-seeker."

For a little time we were all silent. The cover of the shabby old trunk stood open. There was something aged and serene about that trunk. It was as if a presence had come amongst us, and someone from beyond this life had spoken to remind us of the eternal main thing.

M. Trumel was the first to speak and his face was serious:

"That is the original draft of Alphonse Desjardins' prayer. Copies are being made and hung in various offices of the *caisse populaires* throughout the Province of Quebec."

I had to go then, bidding a hurried farewell to my newly made friends in Lévis. I went past the house in which Alphonse Desjardins had lived. I. was gleaming white and graceful in the summer sun. Three maple trees were nodding at the eaves.

I walked down to the dock and took the ferryboat for Quebec. I found running in my mind what I believe is a line that is somewhere in the Bible:

The prayer of the humble man pierceth the clouds.

Author's Note

FOR some time I had known that it was Alphonse Desjardins of Lévis, P.Q., who was the first man in North America to see the need of the common people pooling their thrift and making thereby a credit reservoir from which they could draw at will. But it was not until I spent some time in Quebec that I was able to learn about his early struggles for this creative idea.

It seemed to be worth telling—especially in view of the fact that there are persons in our time who seem to think that all the alternatives and possibilities of democracy have been exhausted. I have tried to tell this story in a somewhat more animated form than would be possible by a straight biography. Hence the method of presentation is that of the novel rather than biography.

Naturally the reader may ask, What of this story really happened? What has been improvised? The answer is that all the important substance of what is here told really happened. A few minor chronological changes, however, have been made. What might be called connective situations have been improvised depicting the effects of Desjardins' thought upon prototype characters, and carrying the story forward. Some minor characters—who are really prototypes—are given fictional names. Such is the case in the chapters about the community I have called Lac Saint André.

As for the main characters—Alphonse, Dorimène, Archbishop Bégin, the priests of the College of Lévis, Earl Grey, and the Hon. Mackenzie King—their parts are as close to real life as was possible to make them. Although the dialogue has been reimagined for the book generally, some passages are documentary.

Shortly after its founding, there were on the Board of Directors of the Caisse Populaire de Lévis: Joseph Verreault, Xavier Marceau, Joseph Gosselin, Pierre Ferland, Jos.-Aug. Carrier, Arcade Cote, A. N. Lemieux, and Theophile Carrier. Credit Committee: Ignace Couture, Napoleon Lamontagne, Thomas Powers, and Jos. Carrier. Supervisory Committee: Francis Labrie, Joseph Delisle, and L. J. Roberge. Alphonse himself, besides, was president and manager, and ex officio a member of the Credit Committee.

In gathering the material out of which this book was written, several journeys were made to points in the Province of Quebec, to Ottawa and elsewhere. I am grateful to the Nova Scotia Cooperative Union and the Nova Scotia Credit Union League for having defrayed the travel expenses of one of these journeys.

I wish to acknowledge especially the assistance of Napoleon Desjardins, the only brother of Alphonse who is still living. He told me many things about his brother's early struggle and creative purpose.

From a newspaper clipping I learned that the chief mourners at the funeral of Alphonse Desjardins were his sons, Raoul Desjardins, manager of the Credit Union of Lévis; Dr. Edgar Desjardins, dentist, of Megantic; Paul Desjardins, civil servant, of Ottawa; and Charles Desjardins; his son-in-law, Mr. Almanzar Lamontagne; his brothers, Mr. L. G. Desjardins, ex-clerk of the Legislative Assembly; Joseph Desjardins, assistant librarian of the Legislative Assembly; Albert Desjardins, of Montreal; and Napoleon Desjardins, civil employee, of Ottawa; his brother-in-law, A. Desjardins, merchant, of Montreal; his nephews, Reverend George Desjardins, parish priest of St. Antoine de Tilly; Emile, Valere, Philippe, and Jean-Marie Desjardins; and E. F. Boisseau, manager of La Banque Nationale at Lévis.

I am indebted to Senator Cyrille Vaillancourt, especially for his articles (in *Revue Desjardins*, 1944), and to Albert Foisy (*Le Canada Français*, January, 1921). Other helpful reading included *Co-operatives Today and Tomorrow*, by George S. Mooney; and the pamphlet, *Alphonse Desjardins*, by Albert Faucher, professor at Laval University, Quebec. Lastly, I am grateful to my wife, Doris Duffy Boyle, for her assistance in various ways.

G. B.